LEADERSHIP
MATRIX
Success in the 21st Century

CASEY TREAT

Leadership Matrix
ISBN 0-931697-45-X
Copyright © 2000 by Casey Treat
Christian Faith International
P. O. Box 98800
Seattle, Washington 98198

Contents

LEADERSHIP
MATRIX

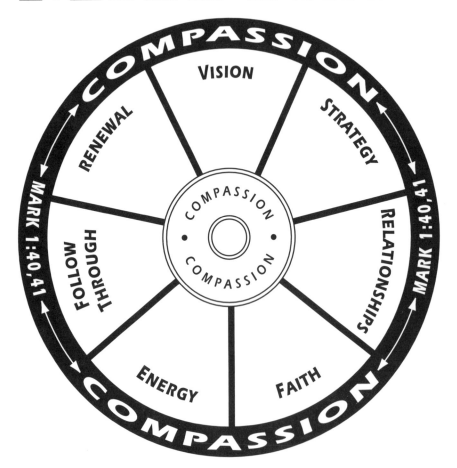

MATRIX (mā'trĭks)

A womb; mold, die or cast from which something is made or manufactured.

Christian Faith International • P.O. Box 98800 • Seattle, WA 98198 • www.caseytreat.org

LEADERSHIP SKILLS AND CHARACTERISTICS THAT CREATE INCREASE

■ VISION
LEADERS CAN SEE WHAT GOD WANTS THEM TO BUILD.
Joshua 6:1,2; Proverbs 29:18

■ STRATEGY
LEADERS KNOW HOW GOD WANTS THEM TO BUILD.
Proverbs 3:19; Psalms 127:1-3

■ RELATIONSHIPS
LEADERS BUILD RELATIONSHIPS THAT HELP THEM FULFILL THEIR DESTINY.
Proverbs 13:20; Acts 15:36

■ FAITH
LEADERS WALK BY FAITH.
Mark 11:22-24; Hebrews 11:6; II Corinthians 5:7

■ ENERGY
LEADERS STAY UP AND LIVE BY THE ENERGY OF THE HOLY SPIRIT.
Philippians 2:13 (AMP); Acts 1:8; John 2:17

■ FOLLOW-THROUGH
LEADERS FOLLOW THROUGH AND OUT LAST THE ENEMY.
Hebrews 10:36-38; James 1:2-4; Matthew 25:21

■ RENEWAL
LEADERS NEVER STOP CHANGING.
Romans 12:2; Colossians 3:9,10; III John 2; Lamentations 3:23

CHAPTER
ONE

Your Role in Leadership

*"From the matrix of My mother
He has made mention of my name."*
Isaiah 49:1b

Every successful person is a leader in some form or fashion. As a born-again believer, you lead yourself in God's Word, in His will and in His plan for your own life. You lead your life through your daily choices, decisions and actions.

As a Christian, you are leading your marriage and your family into the blessings of God, into the will of God and into the good things He has for your lives. In addition, you are leading the people you are around – those you work with, those you commute with, those you eat with, wherever you go. You may not have the title of Manager, Director, Pastor, or Leader, but in reality you are leading people every day of your life by your example, by your spirit, and by your modeling. So regardless of your age, job, or position, you are a leader. You may not be leading people into God's plan, but you are leading them somewhere.

I am convinced that if we will understand our place as Christians, we can be better leaders and rise to a place of influence that will not only help those around us, but it will cause us to live in a more fulfilling, exciting and rewarding way. It will help us to be more like Jesus.

One of the qualities of a leader is that he or she thinks about other people. Did you know that you can't be depressed if you are not thinking about yourself? You can't be discouraged for long if you are not thinking about yourself. You really can't be bitter and angry unless you are focused on yourself. When you get your mind off of yourself, you will feel better and your life will be better.

If every believer would begin to flow in his or her leadership role, not only would we have a great impact on our world, but we would be happier, richer, fuller, and better people ourselves.

I have been praying over leadership for twenty-five years. Before Wendy and I started Christian Faith Center, I was training leaders through leadership classes and seminars to fill the roles of youth pastor, children's pastor, head usher, elder, and all the components that cause a church to function properly.

The first thing a company does is build a leadership team – the chairman, corporate officers, managers, and all of the components that will cause their corporation to function at its best. Once their leadership team is in place, only then do they begin to reach out to their customers.

Often, the Church does just the opposite. We reach out to people, invite them to come to church, then we try to figure out what we are going to do with them. Afterwards, we try to get our leadership team in place, that is not the biblical way to do it.

Jesus started with twelve men. He trained them to be leaders, then He started the Church in Acts, chapter 2.

If you will develop your leadership abilities, you can move into what God has for you. But if you don't *think* like a leader for yourself, your family and your career, you will limit yourself and never experience all that the Lord would like to share with you.

Seven Qualities of Leadership

As I have prayed and sought the Lord about leadership through the years, I have come to the conclusion that *there are seven basic qualities or abilities that must be operating in a successful leader:*

- Vision

- Strategy

- Relationships

- Faith

- Energy

- Follow-Through

- Renewal

These seven things must be in operation for any leader to succeed. If any one of them is not in operation, then there will be problems and struggles.

Many times people say to me, "What is the one thing you have done to cause Christian Faith Center to grow through the years?" There is no answer to that question. "What's the one thing you did to have a happy marriage for twenty years?" There is no answer to that question. "What's the one thing you are doing to raise up successful children?" There is no "one" answer. More than one element is involved to cause success in each of these areas.

Successful leaders do more than one thing right. There is no one thing that will make you a success or make you a great leader in your home, your business, or your ministry.

If we will get the seven basic qualities of leadership operating in various ways and do more than one thing right, we will have success in life. We will see growth. We will experience increase, and we will have prosperity in every area of life.

If you will begin to *think* like a leader, it will change how you deal with your spouse. It will change how you deal with your children. It will change your attitude in your place of employment or ministry, and it will change the results you get.

These seven qualities of leadership are my "Leadership Matrix." As I define and study with you for the rest of this book, realize that we are not born with these skills. They must be learned and developed. Some people are born with leadership gifts, but all of us can learn and grow leadership abilities. You can be the leader God wants you to be and do the good work God wants you to do. The Leadership Matrix will help you do it. Go for it!

Casey Treat

CHAPTER
TWO

Compassion: The Motivating Factor

*Love is the only force with enough power
to move you to godly success.*

The primary motivating factor of every leader must be compassion. In Mark, chapter 1 verses 40-42, Jesus' motivation for healing the leper was compassion:

Now a leper came to Him [Jesus], imploring Him, kneeling down to Him and saying to Him, "If You are willing, You can make me clean." Then Jesus, moved with compassion, stretched out His hand and touched him, and said to him, "I am willing; be cleansed." As soon as He had spoken, immediately the leprosy left him, and he was cleansed.

Whether it's a leper or a person who is poor, someone who is depressed or discouraged, or someone who is in the midst of a marriage failure, the circumstance or the need makes no difference. Anyone who comes to Jesus and says, "I know

You are able," will get the same response: "I am willing."

People in the world say God can do everything, yet they don't believe He is willing. They know He can heal, but they don't believe He is willing. They know He can do miracles, but they don't believe He is willing. One of the reasons is we haven't proclaimed God's will. We have proclaimed our religious traditions. We need to let the world know God is willing because God is love.

Another reason is we haven't always been motivated by the right things. The world is skeptical of the Church, often doubting and critical because of things that have happened and the way we have carried ourselves in the past.

Jesus was moved with compassion. The only motivation that will enable you to be a totally successful leader in your home and in your world is compassion. When the love of God is motivating you, you will succeed.

As humans, we are so quick and so creative, but we are often motivated in a negative way – we use our skills in a wrong way. Husbands can figure out how to manipulate their wives, not because they are moved with compassion, but because they are moved to get what they want. Wives are just as quick and creative: "What do I want and what can I do for my husband to get it?" Far too often we are motivated by our own selfishness rather than by compassion.

Have you ever noticed how kids – these tiny critters, four years old – already know how to manipulate: "Well, Mom said.... What about you, Dad?" Or, "Well, Dad said it was okay. Okay, Mom?" We work people and manipulate circumstances to get what we want.

We go to work to get money only so we can get what we want. Some of us have relationships with people, not because we like the people, but because they are important for us to get what we want. Politics operates that way. Be nice to this one so he or she will vote for you. You vote for them and you get their vote, so it's all about, "What's in it for me?"

Carnal, secular, selfish attitudes that prevail in the world have crept into the Church to a place where we don't realize what is motivating us anymore.

We go to church so we can introduce people to our business. We don't think about hearing from God. We don't think about their soul. We start thinking and looking at everything from the perspective of, "What's in it for me?" We know that people in the world are selfish, but people in the Church can be just as selfish if we're not careful.

When we take an offering in our church, especially if we have a guest preacher who says, "I have a special anointing for you to prosper. I'll touch your offering, pray over it, and if you do this and that, then I will release my anointing and you will get a hundredfold return," the offering will be anywhere from two to ten times as much as a regular offering. When there is the promise of personal gain, the amount goes up. It has happened in our church.

But when we take an offering for poor people, for missions, for the needs of humanity, it's not as much. If the preacher will hype it up and promise a supernatural blessing for their giving, it's like, "Hey, there's something in it for me. I'll be a part of it." But when we have hurting humanity – sighing, crying, and dying – do we give the same?

This isn't being critical. It's just saying we generally get more motivated for personal gain than anything else.

Think about your prayer life. You pray now and then, but when you find out you have cancer, you get serious. You're not teasing now! You are praying! Or when your little one gets sick, you start praying hard.

We pray about the needs of the people in Bulgaria: "Oh, God, help them." In the next breath we ask, "Where are we going for lunch?" But if someone in your house is sick we say, "Pastor, we've got to pray. This is serious." We get much more passionate about personal needs and desires than we do about others' needs.

We need to examine our motivation because it's normal to be more attentive to and more involved with that which is close to us. But have we gotten to a place where our motivation is so self-centered that we're not moved with compassion at all? Are we moved only when there is personal gain?

When Jesus came to earth, there was nothing He didn't have. He is God. He had lived forever in the throne room of heaven. He created the universe. The worlds were spoken into existence out of His mouth. He could create humans, angels, whatever He wanted or needed. But He came as a ransom for you and me. He came to give His life for us. There was nothing for Him to gain personally. He came to seek and to save that which was lost. He did not come to get something for Himself. Jesus was moved with compassion.

I remember reading a theologian's comments as to why healing and miracles occurred in Jesus' ministry. He said, "Jesus did miracles and healed the sick to prove that He was divine, but miracles and healing don't happen anymore because the Lord already established His deity. Miracles and healing passed away after the last apostle died."

I was offended by the manipulating and twisting of God's heart to say that He would use hurting people to prove who He was, that God really didn't care about sick people. To think that God is motivated for personal gain comes from someone with no heart or understanding of God's Word. To think that God uses hurting humanity to promote Himself is incomprehensible, yet how many people today are sitting in churches where their pastors are teaching that miracles and healing have passed away because Jesus did miracles and healing only to prove His deity? Jesus is the same today as He was then, because He is still moved with compassion.

Jesus did miracles because He was moved with compassion. He healed because He was moved with compassion. He taught truth because He was moved with compassion. When He saw the leper in Mark, chapter 1, His heart turned upside down and inside out. He said, "Father, heal the leper." He went to every city and every village healing all manner of sickness and all manner of disease (Matthew 4:23). When He saw the multitudes, He was moved with compassion because they were like sheep without a shepherd (Matthew 9:36). He said to the disciples, "Pray for laborers to go into the harvest fields"(Matthew 9:37,38). That's what motivated Jesus – compassion!

When you and I are motivated with this same love, we will begin to live a higher level of life. Then we will set aside personal gain, wants and needs and start thinking about someone else. It is true that you can't be sad if you aren't thinking about yourself. I'm talking about a lifestyle of sadness and depression. You can't be depressed or fearful if you are not thinking about yourself.

When asked to lead a Home Network meeting, many people respond, "That kind of stuff just makes me nervous." Why? Because you are thinking about you! You aren't thinking about the people you could help. You are asked to be a part of the choir and you respond, "I'd be embarrassed to be up there on the platform." Why? Because you are thinking about you! Instead of being motivated by love, which considers how you can bless other people, your focus is on you. Many Christians never serve in church because they only think about how they will feel or look or be effected.

You can't be bitter, resentful, or angry as long as you are thinking about someone else. You can't even get mad on the freeway if you don't think about yourself. But what happens? Someone pulls in front of you and you are thinking, "How could you do that to me, because I'm the most important person on this whole freeway!" The other person doesn't have a clue that you are there (because he or she is worried only about himself). None of us are thinking about each other. We are thinking about ourselves. This is the way the world operates much of the time.

But what would happen if we would give ourselves a little checkup and ask:

- What's motivating me?

- Why do I do what I do?

- Do I have compassion for people?

If you are moved with love, you have a power, a source, a strength, a motivation that will enable you to be the kind of person that really has an effect on your world. It doesn't take a college education, a genius-level intellect, or a super amount of finances to make a difference. All it takes is a little bit of love!

You can become a special person when you love people. You become a unique individual when the people in your company are looked upon as human beings rather than just as employees. You become a special and valued person when people aren't just numbers, places, positions and titles, but they are people for whom Jesus died. If you are motivated by compassion, you will change your world.

We need to ask ourselves these questions:

- What's the major motivation of my life?

- Do I pray harder when it's for my own needs?

- Am I more inclined to be spiritual when there is something in it for my children or me?

- Do I get more focused and energized when it's for me?

Many will commit to a thirty-year mortgage, but we get offended when the pastor asks us to give to God's house, or make a commitment to the church. We will sacrifice everything to get a couch, a car, a table and dishes, but we don't want to sacrifice anything for someone else. Are we moved with compassion, or are we moved with greed?

The teenagers at Christian Faith Center are cool. They have launched a program where they are putting pictures of all of their unsaved and unchurched friends on a wall in the church. They are going to pray these kids into the Kingdom of God.

As a congregation, we are bringing pictures of our unsaved loved ones and neighbors and we are holding them up before the Lord – not because we want a notch on our gospel pistol, not because we want more numbers in the sanctuary, not just to do what the pastor said to do, and not because we feel some religious guilt that we should do something spiritual. We are doing it because we are moved with compassion.

Religious or Compassionate?

In Galatians, chapter 5, verse 6, Paul says, **For in Christ Jesus neither circumcision nor uncircumcision avails anything, but faith working through love.** He is saying to the church in Galatia, these religious functions, works and activities are not what God cares about.

In many churches today, we try to make everything religious. For instance, clothing. In our church our clothing is pretty relaxed, no big deal. We wear what we want to wear. We want modesty without too much flesh hanging out, but other than that, we don't care what people wear. In some places it's, "The Lord cannot bless you unless you dress properly." What's proper? What is "church clothes"? God doesn't care what you wear. He doesn't look in the catalog to find out what the season's colors are. He doesn't shop. He's not interested. He wears glory. He wears all the colors of the rainbow. God isn't looking at your clothes, and we shouldn't be worried about what each other is wearing.

We try to look at makeup as spiritual or unspiritual. "God doesn't want you wearing this," or "He wants you wearing that." He could not care less. Put on your war paint if you want to!

We try to make something spiritual of our hair. I know one church that teaches, "If a man's hair is long, it's evil, and if a woman's hair is short, it's evil." Come on! Thank God if you have any hair! If you don't have any, go buy some! Of course, if you're bald that just means the glory is coming through and you've got more room for all the brains inside there!

We try to make many things an issue and God isn't a bit concerned about it. He doesn't care. He's not interested. It's irrelevant. Circumcised or uncircumcised – the Lord isn't interested in these natural, worldly, carnal things.

If it affects your spirituality, then the Lord becomes interested. If it begins to hurt, hinder, or affect your life, the Lord becomes interested. But in the theological, biblical sense, God could not care less.

But here is what He does care about: **faith working through love** (Galatians 5:6). That's what He cares about. Faith working through love. God is interested in your faith, but only if it is motivated by love.

The Amplified Bible makes it a little clearer: **faith activated and energized and expressed and working through love.** That's what God cares about: Faith motivated, activated, energized, expressed, and working through love. I believe that many of our faith projects fail because our motive isn't love.

We are praying for ourselves, for our own gain, for our own desires, but there is little or no motivation of compassion. We pray to look good or to be big! We are praying to get a new position, but God doesn't answer prayers motivated by our own ego! God will move in response to your prayers when you care about people.

Jesus, moved with compassion, stretched out His hand and said to the leper, "I am willing." The leper was cleansed. The need was met. The circumstance was changed.

As we go through this leadership matrix, I pray that we will understand and remember whatever we're doing, the motivation has got to be love. Whatever we do, the energy behind it has to be compassion.

19

Selfishness, fear, anger or ego do not have enough power to move you to godly success. Only the love of God is strong enough to take us through the challenges of life and make us leaders that really make a difference. You can prosper and have good success if you get motivated by the power of God's love.

CHAPTER

THREE

Vision

Your vision is your future,
your future is in your heart.

T he word "matrix" literally means a womb, a mold, a die or cast from which something is manufactured. With a matrix you can create any part or any component in the manufacturing world. In the computer world, they use the term "matrix" to define a program or a system that is used to develop different products. A matrix is simply that womb or that place where the ingredients are placed to produce results in your life. Isaiah 49:1 says,**"Listen, O coastlands to Me, and take heed, you peoples from afar! The Lord has called Me from the womb; from the matrix of My mother He has made mention of My name."**

If you get this leadership matrix working in your heart and you get these ingredients active and alive in your life, you will produce greater results. We are going to fine tune each of these ingredients and improve them. Then you will have more influence and success, which will produce more prosperity and joy in every aspect of your life and the lives of others.

The first thing we will look at in the leadership matrix is *vision*. Vision enables you to see what God wants you to build. It is used to see into your future. God wants us to live with vision. Where there is no vision people fail.

Another word for vision is *hope*, which is the ability to see something positive in your future. You have a hope for a good marriage, happy kids and a successful company. Where there is no hope, people perish.

Hebrews 11:1 says, **Now faith is the substance of things hoped for....** Many people have faith in God, but they aren't producing any results. The reason is because they have no hope. They have faith – "I know God can do it. I trust Him. I'm believing God" – but they are not doing anything because there is no hope, no vision.

Without hope or vision, you have nothing to use your faith for. Remember, faith will not work just to feed the desires of your flesh. If all you are doing is using your faith so you can get a more comfortable car, a bigger TV set or to fulfill your fleshly desires, your faith won't work. Faith in God was not designed for you to get fatter and die younger!

Your faith will work when it is anchored in hope – hope for a better future. Hope that is moved with compassion. Hope for something exciting and rewarding. When your job, home and family are a part of a godly hope or vision, your faith will work.

We must have a desire to live a life with vision, which is purpose and destiny, so that when we stand before the Father, He will say, **"Well *done*, good and faithful servant..."** (Matthew 25:21).

When you live with vision, your faith will work and your life will be effective and creative, impacting and changing your world.

I'm not saying that we're all going to be apostles and national leaders. But we are all called to help others – someone on your job, in your neighborhood, at your school and the moms, dads, and kids in your world.

If you keep touching one, two, three and four people, then at the end of your life there will be a group of people who will say, "Thank God that person was alive! Thank God he or she had compassion and vision and used their life for something good!"

The reason God wants us to walk in the Spirit is not so that you don't do all the fleshly things, but that you *know God's will, you have a vision, and you see your future.*

Acts 2:17 says: **'And it shall come to pass in the last days, says God, that I will pour out of My Spirit on all flesh; your sons and your daughters shall prophesy, your young men shall see visions, your old men shall dream dreams.'**

The result of the outpouring of God's Spirit on all flesh is not just speaking with tongues, not just healing miracles, not just signs and wonders. The result of the outpouring of the Holy Spirit is first of all, *young men shall see visions and old men shall dream dreams.*

You begin to see into tomorrow. You are not living just for today. You are not an animal trying to survive. You go beyond making a living. You are created in the likeness and image of God with a vision for the future.

Habakkuk, chapter 2, verse 2 says, **Write the vision and make it plain on tablets, that he may run who reads it.**

Every day of my life I carry with me a vision for my entire life written out in a section of my notebook. I have listed things that I am working on right now, the vision for my current days, then the vision of what I will be working on in the near future and for the next five to ten years. I also have written down what I will accomplish by the end of my life. I have written out how many years I am going to have to live to accomplish what I'm to do.

So many people are saying, "I hope that I'll be alive." Well, you probably won't be because of Proverbs 29:18 (KJV): **Where there is no vision, the people perish....**

Where does your vision stop? Are you thinking, "When I'm sixty-five, I'm going to get me a Winnebago and go down to Arizona"? If so, we'll start preparing your funeral as soon as you buy that Winnebago, because that's the end of your vision.

Years ago, I had a wonderful friend who was a truck driver, but he hated his job. He ended up on that job because it was a good way to make a living, but he had no vision. When you have no vision, you always end up with jobs you don't like. Instead of living a destiny, you just make a living. This man was on the road for hours and hours at a time and he despised it. He said, "When I'm sixty-five I'm going to retire and relax." Within six weeks after he stopped driving, he was dead. He had no vision for anything after retirement.

Your anointed imagination must be developed so you can see your future.

A Visionary "Sees" Before Manifestation

Joshua, chapter 6, verses 1 and 2 say: **Now Jericho was securely shut up because of the children of Israel; none went out, and none came in. And the Lord said to Joshua: "See! I have given Jericho into your hand, its king, and the mighty men of valor."**

Verse 1 says Jericho was shut up, on guard, its gates were closed, and no one was coming in or going out. Verse 2 says that God had given it into Joshua's hand. Which one is true? Was it shut up, ready for battle? Or, was it already conquered and in Joshua's hand?

If you are a visionary, you understand that both are true. In the natural, Jericho's gates were closed and they were ready to fight. But in the spirit, Joshua saw it as already conquered. In his anointed imagination, he saw that he had overcome the enemy.

You and I must develop this skill to be able to see something before it happens. We can do that in a variety of ways. If you see a hairstyle that you like, you can pay $50 and have it put on your head! If you see an outfit you like, you can try it on, buy it and wear it. You have the ability to see it before it happens in certain areas, but you need to develop that for all aspects of your life.

Most of us don't grow up with a vision for our life. The Lord can use circumstances and we pray for God to direct our steps. But I think many of us are just bumping along and not living with purpose.

Do you go to the grocery store and buy whatever you think you need, or do you write out a list first? If my wife,

Wendy, asks me to go to the grocery store to pick up three things, usually I'll come back with ten things and I'll probably forget at least one of the three items she asked me to get.

As I watch people walk around the grocery store, most of the time I see people with a list. Now, isn't it amazing that many people won't go to the grocery store without a list, but most of us go into adult life without a vision. We have never written down anything that we believed we were gifted or called to do and that we planned and purposed to accomplish. We get up every morning, go to work and hope for the best.

What are you getting up every day to accomplish? "I just want to find some clothes that are ironed and get to work on time." Is that all? You've got to have a higher purpose than that.

I'll never forget my pastor friend looking at a beautiful mansion up in the hills of his city. He said to the Lord, "I cannot imagine living in a house like that." The Lord spoke back in his spirit and said, "It's okay. You never will." A few minutes later he said, "Wait a minute. That's not nice. How come I never will?" The Lord said, "Because you can't imagine it."

Wendy and I built a new house, which we worked on for several years. Recently, our kids were talking to the neighbor kids. These kids said to my children, "Our dad said your dad is too rich." These people don't have a clue if someone gave us the property, or if a builder blessed us with this home. But the neighbor's vision is, "I am poor and other people are rich."

In other words, there's something wrong with anyone who has what he doesn't have. He has put this kind of thinking into his kids. Maybe you were raised this way: "Those rich people are only rich because they are greedy and evil," or, "They got it from their parents. We are the 'real people.' We are honest and clean. That's why we're poor." They may not have said those exact words, but that's the message.

What happens when you have a vision? What happens if you begin to see something? Personally, I'm going to live at the highest level so I can be an example of Jesus. I want to show people what a Christian life of honesty and integrity is all about. The world is not impressed when they see Christians struggling and taking up $5 offerings. But they take notice when they see a godly man or woman with the blessing of the Lord upon their life. People of the world then say, "There's a person of influence – someone who can lead and make a difference!"

Some people have said, "I'm happy with my life just the way it is, and I'm really not too concerned with anything else." This goes back to our primary motivation. Can you really be happy if all that matters to you is getting what *you* want?

What if you begin to care about lost and dying humanity? What if you begin to give, serve and bring people into your house and change their lives? That takes vision. There is no vision for a life of survival – just making it through and being happy with what you've got. But if you will begin to see what you can do to make a difference in your world, in your company, in your ministry, or in your Home Network meeting, suddenly there will be motivation and fulfillment that doesn't come any other way.

Refocusing Your Lens

In Matthew 6:22,23 Jesus said: **"The lamp of the body is the eye. If therefore your eye is good, your whole body**

27

will be full of light. But if your eye is bad, your whole body will be full of darkness. If therefore the light that is in you is darkness, how great is that darkness!"

Notice, Jesus said, "The lamp of the body is the eye." Your eye represents your vision – what you see ahead. If your eye is seeing good things – a positive life and an exciting, good future – then your whole life is in the light. Your whole life has the light turned on!

But if your eye is bad, if you see dark days, if you're afraid of the future, if you have a negative outlook, your whole life is dark. "Well, you know, if the marriage doesn't work, I can always get a divorce." "If this job doesn't work out, I'll just quit and go somewhere else." If you have that kind of negative, pessimistic outlook, your whole life is dark. Your vision will control your life, and if your life is dark it's because your vision is negative.

I'm not saying there are always positive, happy things going on in the world. There are negative things, there are accidents and crises, but that doesn't mean you should focus on them and build your life around them. Every marriage has a few challenges, but don't focus on them and build your life around them. Instead, build on the strengths and focus on the positive qualities of your spouse.

When you were dating, all you saw were the good qualities in that person's life. Now, after ten years of marriage, all you see is what is bad. Your vision is the challenge. The person hasn't changed. Your vision has changed and you are focusing on the problems.

If you point your camera at ugly stuff, all of your pictures are going to be of ugly stuff! Many of us have pointed our lens on the negatives of the world, the negatives of our spouse, the negatives of our job, the negatives of everything around us. We start our day complaining about the traffic and we end the day complaining about something else. Everything in between is negative as well. Then, when we look at the photo album of our life, we wonder why all the pictures are ugly!

While you may be frustrated at some of the circumstances around you, listen to the Lord. He is still there. He hasn't left you. Choose to focus the lens of your life on that which is good, on that which is right, on what God has put in your heart and on the opportunities and the possibilities that are ahead of you! Look with a clear, positive vision, and your whole life will be full of light. You'll start getting back some great pictures!

Perhaps your vision is blurry. You believe you see something that the Lord has for you, but you're not sure what it is. Get focused. Get a clear vision of where you're going and as you develop that vision, you will move into God's will for your life.

God gives vision, but that doesn't mean you are to sit around and wait for Him to make it clear in your mind. Begin to move into what you desire and into what you believe and begin to develop your vision. As you do that, the Lord will enable you, empower you and He will help you.

In every part of our walk with God, He never does it for us, but He always does it with us.

I've talked to so many people who have been saved for years. I ask them, "Do you know your future? Do you know your destiny?" They often say, "Well, I'm not sure. I'm waiting on the Lord and He hasn't said a word."

That kind of attitude says, "It's all up to God. God has to tell me what to do." God doesn't respond to that. You are not a victim. You are not an animal who needs someone to take care of you. You are not a being without potential. God will not treat you like a baby. He will only respond to your faith, to your steps, to your forward momentum. You are made in His image, He cannot deal with you like a puppet or helpless creature.

Forward Momentum

The Bible says the Holy Spirit is our Helper, not our baby-sitter! It's like the person who says, "Well, I don't speak with tongues." Why not? "I'm waiting for the Lord." God doesn't speak with tongues. *You do!* The Bible said the Holy Spirit will help *you* as you begin to pray, as you speak out of your heart, as you take the step of faith to let the prayer language come out of *your* mouth. Then God will empower it and anoint it. And so it is as you step out with a vision and faith that God will lead you.

When I was nineteen years old, my pastor asked me to teach in a Home Network ministry at our church. He said, "I have a group of pot smokers and drug addicts and I want you to be their Home Network leader."

I was brand new in the Lord, but he sensed the call of God on my life. I'm sure he figured I couldn't mess these people up anyway because they were already so far gone!

I went to their apartment for the first meeting. They had bean bag chairs and black lights. I said to myself, "I thought I left all this, and here I am back in it – but this time I've got my Bible."

I began to minister to them, but I was nervous that I would do something wrong. I felt God's calling on my life, and I had the beginning of a vision for my future. But I was afraid I would make a mistake.

I went to my pastor and said, "What if I do something wrong?" He said, "You cannot steer a bike until you get it rolling." That's a very simplistic illustration, yet it has never left me. Get rolling and God will steer you. He may need to turn you right or left, but at least He can turn you if you are moving! But if you aren't doing anything, there is no way you can develop a vision for your future.

Begin to move toward the vision to which God has called you.

CHAPTER
FOUR

Strategy

We don't need more power,
we need to know what to do
with the power we have.

The second part of the leadership matrix is strategy. Vision is "what we are going to do," and strategy is "how we're going to do it." An effective leader has a strategy to fulfill the plan of God in his or her life.

Let's look at Proverbs, chapter 3, verses 13-16. As we read these verses, think in terms of the "how" to accomplish your vision and fulfill your hopes and dreams:

Happy is the man who finds wisdom, and the man who gains understanding; For her proceeds are better than the profits of silver, and her gain than fine gold. She is more precious than rubies, and all the things you may desire cannot compare with her. Length of days is in her right hand, in her left hand riches and honor.

Wisdom is the key element in your strategy plans. While some people say, "I just need more money," wisdom will bring you the money. Or, "I just don't have time. I'm getting too old." No, the length of your days is tied in with wisdom.

Verse 19 says, **The Lord by wisdom founded the earth; by understanding He established the heavens.** How are you going to birth and establish your company, your family, and your ministry? By wisdom and understanding.

Just because you have a vision doesn't mean you will fulfill it. If a person has a vision from the Lord and he or she is asked, "How are you going to fulfill it?" they might respond, "I'm just going to let the Lord do it."

Get out of that pseudo-spiritual mode. That's not a spiritual way of thinking. God does not live your life – you do!

Recently I was with a fellow who has been married just over a year. He said, "I can't love my wife. I just can't do it. I know the Lord will love her through me." That sounds real spiritual, right? "I'll just let the Lord love her through me."

I said, "Brother, the only problem with that is, the Bible says, **Husbands, love your wives, just as Christ loved the church and gave Himself for it** (Ephesians 5:25). God is not sleeping with her! While He does love her as a daughter, He told you to love her as your wife." This man said, "Oh, that's a bummer! I never thought of that!"

Many times when we think we are being spiritual, we have become pseudo-spiritual. We make excuses.

If you have a vision to be a real estate agent, what's your strategy? Are you going to sell residential or commercial property? Are you going to focus in one small area, or are you going to try to service an entire region? How are you going to advertise? How are you going to get your clientele? What is your plan – the "how to" – to fulfill your vision of becoming a real estate agent?

If your vision is to build a family, how are you going to do it? What kind of school are you going to put your kids in? What is your strategy, your plan? How are you going to make sure those kids grow up to be godly and successful? "Well, I'm just going to turn them over to the Lord." No! The Lord told *you* to raise them up in the nurture and admonition of the Lord (see Ephesians 6:4).

Happy is the man [or woman] **who finds wisdom, and the man** [or woman] **who gains understanding** (Proverbs 3:13). That's how you become established and that's how you prosper in every area of your life.

Let's Be Wiser Than the "Sons of This World"

In Luke, chapter 16, Jesus tells a story of a steward who made some mistakes, but he was a wise man. Let's read verses 1-8, paying particular attention to verse 8:

"There was a certain rich man who had a steward, and an accusation was brought to him that this man was wasting his goods. So he called him and said to him, 'What is this I hear about you? Give an account of your stewardship, for you can no longer be a steward.' Then the steward said within himself, 'What shall I do? For my master is taking the stewardship away from me. I cannot dig; I am ashamed to beg. I have resolved what to do, that when I am put out of the

stewardship, they may receive me into their houses.' So he called every one of his master's debtors to him, and said to the first, 'How much do you owe my master?' And he said, 'A hundred measures of oil.' So he said to him, 'Take your bill, and sit down quickly and write fifty.' Then he said to another, 'And how much do you owe?' So he said, 'A hundred measures of wheat.' And he said to him, 'Take your bill, and write eighty.' So the master commended the unjust steward because he had dealt shrewdly [or wisely]. **For the sons of this world are more shrewd in their generation than the sons of light."**

In the development of your strategy, learn everything you can from the world. You are not a part of the world, but you are in it and you can use the knowledge and wisdom that they have. Don't be some pseudo-spiritual dummy that says, "God's going to do it." No! The children of this world are wiser in their generation than God's children are. So we need to plug in and learn everything we can.

We've had people come to my church, Christian Faith Center, for the first time, and they said things like, "I don't understand why you have all those electrical instruments and microphones. You've got TV's in church, and church announcements on TV. What's up? Then, in your youth department, you've got video games, lights, smoke, sound and all that stuff. What's up?"

In their church, they are still functioning as if it's the 1600s! They are speaking in Latin and wondering why no one says "Amen!"

The sons of this world are more shrewd [wiser] **in their generation than the sons of light** (Luke 16:8). We're not to be like them, but we are to gain wisdom that we can use to fulfill the purposes of God. Jesus is the One who said this, so as you develop your strategy, learn from everything around you. Be wise in your planning and preparation, then God will bring success.

In the next chapter, we will look at the third area of the leadership matrix – *relationships*. You're not the Lone Ranger, but just in case you think you are – even he needed Tonto!

FIVE

Relationships

*Our relationships with people show the strength or weakness
of our spiritual life.*

The third leadership component is *relationships*. Relationships enable us to function as the Body of Christ and to fulfill our destiny.

On the most basic level, we need a good relationship with God, with our spouse, with our kids, and with people who will enable us to move forward in God's calling on our lives.

In God's Kingdom, there are no lone rangers, no islands, no individuals who do it all. Anyone who doesn't need anyone else will be seriously limited in fulfilling the will of God.

Even in the natural world, people skills are more important than technical skills. Through the years I've known many people who had great technical skills, but their people skills were so bad that no one wanted to work with them. They were great in terms of knowledge and ability, but the general attitude was, "Go somewhere else. We don't want to be around you."

So no matter how much vision and strategy you have, if you don't have good people skills – the ability to relate and build good relationships – you are seriously limited.

There are people today that I watch. I see their work, I see their discipline, and I see their desire, yet they just offend everybody. I mean, they are like an onion in the refrigerator. It smells everything up! And you just can't fulfill your destiny if the people around you don't want you to succeed, and if you don't want them to succeed. Good relationships are the key to success.

Proverbs 18, verse 1, says, **A man** [or woman] **who isolates himself seeks his own desire; he rages against all wise judgment.**

Isolation says, "I don't need anybody. All I need is God. Just me and God." God said, **He who does not love his brother whom he has seen, how can he love God whom he has not seen?** (1 John 4:20). So you can't separate relationship with God and relationship with people.

Jesus said: **"'You shall love the Lord your God with all your heart, with all your soul, and with all your mind.' This is the first and great commandment. And the second is like it: 'You shall love your neighbor as yourself'"** (Matthew 22:37-39).

You can't love God without loving people, and if you isolate yourself, you will rage against wisdom, which obviously means you will not fulfill the will of God in your life. So we need to improve our skills in building relationships. We must become "people" people!

I've had people say to me, "I come to church and no one says 'Hi' to me." Sometimes I want to react and say something smart back to them! Usually I don't, but relationships are a great manifestation of the eternal principle, "You reap what you sow."

Proverbs 18:24 says, **A man who has friends must himself be friendly....** So if you are in a crowd of Christians and you don't have any friends, guess what? You need to take off that big sign, which says, "Get away from me." You will keep reaping what you sow. "Yeah, but you don't know what I've been through." No, I probably don't. "I've been hurt." I'm sure you have. "I've been abused." I understand that. "Nobody treats me right." So you're going to spend the rest of your life judging and punishing Christians for what others did to you? Is that how you are going to live? You're going to hate everybody the rest of your life because of what someone did to you? If you think like a victim, you will always set yourself up to be hurt.

You have to decide, "I'm going to be a people person, and the only way to fulfill my destiny is to get involved with people." That is why we have women's Bible studies and breakfasts, men's Bible studies and breakfasts and Network meetings. Then, if you come to our church and you say, "I don't have any friends," what you're really saying is, "I don't want any friends." We are working hard to try to get people involved with people so they will let down their defenses and get close to others.

At Christian Faith Center we have 500 families that are inviting members of our church to come over every month. "No one ever invites me." I'm telling you, 500 families wish you would show up at their house! "I didn't know anything about it." It's in the bulletin, it's on the big screen, and I'm screaming about it at every service! Obviously, you have built a life that isolates and that doesn't provide an opportunity for

41

the development of relationships. You've got to pull down those defenses and say, "I cannot fulfill my destiny if I don't get close to people."

We must be open and desirous of relationships with all kinds of people. God will use them to move us in His will. As we help others, they help us and we all get to destiny.

Many Members But One Body

In First Corinthians 12:12, Paul talks about the Church and our relationships as church members: **For as the body is one and has many members, but all the members of that one body, being many, are one body, so also is Christ.** There are many members in the Body of Christ, but we are all one.

Just like the physical body has shoulders, arms, elbows, wrists, hands, fingers, feet, toes, and ankles – all kinds of members – there is only one body. The Body of Christ is one, but it has all kinds of parts. We flow together as one.

For by one Spirit we were all baptized into one body... (v. 13). When you were born again, the Holy Spirit put you in the Body of Christ. **Whether Jews or Greeks, whether slaves or free....** This is an important part. Once you become a member of this Body, you are no longer a Jew or a Gentile. You are no longer bond or free. You are no longer black or white, or Asian or Hispanic. You are no longer Swedish, Norwegian, Asian, African, or American. We are one **and have all been made to drink into one Spirit** (v. 13).

I'm not trying to deny your cultural heritage. If you like to celebrate it, that's fine. But in your attitude towards life, you are not a Swedish Christian. You are not a Norwegian Christian. You are not a Bulgarian Christian. You are not a Messianic Christian. You are not an American Christian. This is not a black church, and neither is it a white or a red church. Anything that separates us from people or that puts up a wall is contrary to Christ.

By focusing on color of skin or cultural differences, we are tearing down the relationships that God wants us to have.

Obviously, you may have been through things that I don't understand, and I've been through things that you don't understand. You have words that I don't say and I have words that you don't say, but that's the fun of all of us being mixed up together!

The fun of having peanut butter and chocolate is to stir them up! That's what I'm saying. Let's put them both in the same bowl and see what kind of cookies we can get out of this deal!

Some people ask, "Are you going to that black church?" or, "Are you going to that white church?" "I heard that church has a lot of black things going on." What does that mean? Or, "I heard that church has a white pastor." What about the "saved" pastor?

Someone said to me, "Brother Casey, we've been having a lot of black music in this church." I said, "I hadn't noticed any colors coming off the platform. Is there a color code for music? Something I'm unaware of?" This is the type of mentality that destroys relationships. It's that small mentality that centers on their prejudices, hurts, and their past, which keeps them from their future.

No Distinctions!

Paul said that we are all baptized into one Body. No more Jews, no more Gentiles, no more bond, no more free, no more rich, no more poor, no more nationalities, no more races, but one new person in Christ.

Verse 14 of First Corinthians 12 says, **For in fact the body is not one member but many.**

On January 6th of the new millennium Wendy and I celebrated our twentieth anniversary in ministry. We had a big banquet downtown and acted like big shots! Drs. Fred and Betty Price who pastor Crenshaw Christian Center in Los Angeles were there. Fred ordained Wendy and me. For all these years, he has said I'm his white son. He says, "It would be impossible for a black man and a black woman to come together in holy matrimony and conceive and bring forth a white child. However, in the Spirit...." Then he goes through this description of how a black man can have a white son in the Lord.

If you think about it, when the members in your body were born, they were all part of one body. You didn't have a black foot and a white hand. When I'm with Pastor Price, I'm not white or black. I'm just part of the Body.

For in fact the body is not one member but many [we're many members, but one body]. **If the foot should say, "Because I am not a hand, I am not of the body," is it therefore not of the body? If the ear should say, "Because I am not an eye, I am not of the body," is it therefore not of the body? If the whole body were an eye, where would be the hearing? If the whole were hearing, where would be the smelling? But now God has set the members, each one of them, in the body just as He pleased. And if they were all one member, where would the body be? But now indeed there are many members, yet one body. And the eye cannot say to the hand, "I have no**

44

need of you"; nor again the head to the feet, "I have no need of you." No, much rather, those members of the body which seem to be weaker are necessary (1 Corinthians 12:14-22).

Paul continues to compare the physical body and its many parts to the Body of Christ. Though there are many members, there is one Body. He says, **Those members of the body which we think to be less honorable, on these we bestow greater honor...** (v. 23). In other words, we protect and care for them. And so it must be in the Church.

Becoming "People" People

The point is, we must become "people" people. We are to care about people, to relate to people and to live for people. We're not envious or jealous and we're not picking on each other. We're not competing with each other. We're not gossiping about each other. We're helping each other achieve God's best.

Many of us are frustrated because we have the "pie mentality" of life, meaning, "I've got to have the biggest slice before you get part of my slice. When I see you eating a big slice, I get mad because it means I get a smaller slice of the pie."

But the Bible does not say that life is a pie. It says life is a river. You can drink as much as you want. God is infinite. He's not going to run dry. There's more than enough for all of us to get everything we want. I don't have to worry about you getting too much, because we can both get as much as we want.

The reason people get envious and jealous is because they think somebody got a piece of their pie. Many of us

45

were raised with this mentality. Remember sitting at the dinner table and hearing, "Eat those carrots, because some people in Africa don't have any carrots. Be grateful for yours and eat them all."

The message was, "You took some of theirs, and if you waste yours, it's going to cost them." Whether you clean your plate up or not, does not affect what the people in Africa eat. It has nothing to do with that. Some say, "We throw away so much food, we could feed a whole country." No, you couldn't because that country can only eat what their leaders and the vision of the people receive. It has nothing to do with what America throws away. That "pie mentality" is a misnomer.

Life is a river. Everyone drinks as much as they want, but the enemy's tactic is to get you into jealousy, competition, and comparing. "My neighbor got a new car. I suppose he thinks he's cool and a big shot now! He probably won't even wave at me anymore."

If we do not function well in the Body of Christ, we are like a handicapped person. When a physical body is handicapped, there's one part that's not doing its job, either because of an accident or a birth defect. I have a little friend named Jordan Willis who cannot do what the normal person can do. He is developmentally disabled or retarded. He is held back from achieving his maximum potential.

Any Christian who is envious or jealous, who gossips or competes, who gets angry when others are accomplishing great things, is handicapped. They are a retarded part of the Body. I'm not trying to be politically incorrect! I'm simply trying to make a point.

When you say, "Now, who do they think they are? I heard that pastor drives a Mercedes," or, "I saw someone the other day who was put on the stage at church. I should be up there on that stage." Competition. Jealousy. Envy.

I'm trying to illustrate what a lack of relational skills will do to you. You are just dragging your body around. You don't get out of your little shell. You don't get out of your little attitude. You don't get out of your fear and bitterness and build relationships and start loving people.

Your relationship skills will decide your destiny. Whether you are in business, ministry, teaching, manufacturing, or engineering, your relationship skills will decide your destiny.

Wendy and I treat every person like a member of our church. Sometimes people don't like us because they've heard things or someone told them something. But we treat them all like they are members of our church. "Oh, it's good to see you. I missed you last Sunday. What do you mean, 'I've never been to your church'? That's why I missed you! When are you going to come?"

Embrace every person you meet. They may be a part of your future. Love God and love all His kids. When you meet a negative person, be kind and move on. Never let a closed, bitter, or small attitude keep you from people. If you can't love people, you can't love God.

Just love people. Drop your rocks and build relation-ships. It's a key to your future.

47

Faith

*Faith is a lifestyle of confidence and trust in God,
not a doctrine or a theology.*

Romans 1:17b says, **The just shall live by faith.** This same verse is found in three additional places in the Bible: Habakkuk 2:4; Galatians 3:11; and Hebrews 10:38. We walk by faith, not by sight. That means our decisions are controlled by what we believe, not by what we feel or see in the natural sense.

Faith is so important to God. We fight the good fight of faith. We pray the prayer of faith. We walk by faith. We overcome by faith. God is watching for faith. He responds to faith. He doesn't respond to need, complaints, or cries. He responds to faith.

If you were to ask people, "Do you have faith?" many would respond, "Oh, yes, I have strong faith." Yet they don't really know what faith is from a biblical perspective.

Let's look at two aspects of faith: What is it? And are we using faith in our lifestyle so we have the matrix to bring forth success and victory, to be the person God has called us to be and do the things God has called us to do?

Faith Is Manifested in Your Words

In Mark, chapter 11, Jesus gave an illustrated sermon. He spoke to a fig tree because it did not have any fruit on it. He went to a fig tree looking for fruit and there was nothing there, so He spoke to it and said, **"Let no one eat fruit from you ever again"** (Mark 11:14).

Then Jesus and His disciples went into Jerusalem, preached in the temple, and went back to Bethany to stay that night. The next morning they were on their way back into Jerusalem. The disciples saw the tree Jesus had cursed, and Peter said, **"Rabbi, look! The fig tree which You cursed has withered away"** (v. 21). Then Jesus said, **"Have faith in God"** (v. 22).

Was the Lord saying, "You need to have faith so you can talk to trees?" No, that's not the point. The illustration was, when there is something in your life that does not produce fruit, when something is happening that isn't productive, when something is going on that isn't what you want, use faith. Have faith in God. Faith is manifested in what you say.

In verse 23 Jesus goes on to say, **"For assuredly, I say to you, whoever says to this mountain…."** Whether it's a tree or a mountain, the point is, there is something in your life that isn't the way you want it to be. There's a circumstance, a need, or a situation. He uses the tree and the mountain in His illustration, but faith is His focus.

Jesus was saying, "When there are circumstances in front of you, speak to them. In verse 23, Jesus shows us how and what to speak to our mountains: **"'Be removed and be cast into the sea,' and does not doubt in his heart, but believes that those things he says will be done, he will have whatever he says."**

That is how you use faith. Faith is not having a warm, fuzzy feeling while you watch "Touched by an Angel." This is a very misunderstood area, and because we're not using our faith in many situations, we're getting ripped off. We don't have the ingredients to bring forth the kind of lifestyle that God wants us to have and we're missing out.

If you miss an ingredient when you are making a cake, it's not going to be right when you pull it out of the oven. You think, Oh, boy, this is going to be good. You sink your teeth into it and it's not what you expected!

I hate it when I forget to put salt in my oatmeal. I'm all excited about breakfast and with the first spoonful, I think, "This is bland. No salt."

You may be trying to enjoy life, healing, prosperity, marriage, parenting and career and you keep getting this bland feeling. You keep getting this "blah" thing going on in your life. You are struggling with weight, with finances and with relationships. You aren't producing the kind of fruit that you want, so you pray a little bit and come to church a little bit and do a few things.

You ask, "Why aren't my circumstances changing? What is it going to take?" You've got to start speaking to your circumstances. You've got to use your faith. Faith is the one ingredient in the Leadership Matrix that causes you to change negative circumstances to positive ones.

Jesus says, "When I spoke to the tree, guys, I showed you how to use your faith in God. Speak to your mountain, don't doubt in your heart, believe that what you say will come to pass and you will have what you say."

Notice, you don't have what you want. You don't have what you hope. You don't have what you wish. You have what you say. That's faith. Believing and speaking.

Believing and Speaking

Let's use salvation as an illustration. How did you get saved? You believed in your heart that Jesus is Lord and that God raised Him from the dead; then you confessed with your mouth that Jesus is Lord.

Romans, chapter 10, verses 9 and 10 say:

If you confess with your mouth the Lord Jesus and believe in your heart that God has raised Him from the dead, you will be saved. For with the heart one believes unto righteousness, and with the mouth confession is made unto salvation.

In Matthew 10:32 Jesus said: **"Therefore whoever confesses Me before men, him I will also confess before My Father who is in heaven."**

So both your heart and your mouth are involved in getting saved: Believe in your heart and confess with your mouth. When you believed that Jesus is Lord and you confessed His lordship in your life, you were saved.

The moment you were saved, did you see the Lamb's Book of Life and see the angel write your name in the Book? No! Did you see the throne room of God and Jesus sitting at His right hand, saying to the Father, "Here's another one, Lord. They're coming in"? You didn't see that. Did you see the angels rejoice? The Bible says, **"There will be more joy in heaven over one sinner who repents than over ninety-nine just persons who need no repentance"** (Luke 15:7).

I didn't see angels rejoicing. I didn't even feel the brush of angels' wings. I didn't see or feel anything. Yet people walk out of that prayer room or kitchen or wherever they were and say, "I'm a Christian. I've been born again." They believe that if they died right then, they would go to heaven because the Bible says, **To be absent from the body** [is] **to be present with the Lord** (2 Corinthians 5:8).

The same faith you used to be born again – believing and confessing – can be used for healing. You believe Jesus is your Healer, and you say with your mouth, "Jesus is my Healer. I call my back healed. I am healed in the name of Jesus. I call my head healed. I believe I receive healing in the name of Jesus."

When someone asks, "How are you doing?" you can say, "I believe I am healed." Why walk around saying, "My back is killing me"? Use your faith.

Many times I've prayed for healing and didn't feel any better, but I didn't feel any better when I got saved either. But I got saved by faith. Use your faith for healing in the same way: Believe with your heart and confess with your mouth.

If you walk around talking about "my headache," "my heart problem," "my rheumatoid arthritis," "my bad knee," "my sore back," your big mouth will kill you and you will keep having what you say!

If you say what you've got instead of what you want, you get more of what you've got instead of what you want. Use your faith.

Why not use your faith for finances just like you did for salvation? When you were born again, you confessed Jesus as Lord and you believed in your heart that God raised Him from the dead.

Why not confess, "Jesus is my Provider. I believe in my heart He is Jehovah Jireh, the Lord Who Provides, and I receive His financial blessings"? Paul said, **And my God shall supply all your need according to His riches in glory by Christ Jesus** (Philippians 4:19). That's not just the need for survival. That means need concerning anything that God has put in your life to accomplish.

I'm not going to say, "Well, I can't afford it. I wish. I wonder. You never know." No, I'm going to say, "My God supplies all my need according to His riches in glory by Christ Jesus. Jehovah Jireh provides more than enough for every good work." Say it with your mouth, believe it in your heart, and your faith will bring finances to you.

"Well, brother, I'm hoping the union will get me that extra quarter raise." Is that where your faith is? Thank God for the natural things that companies, unions and banks do. We live in a natural world and we use those things, but our faith is in God. Have faith in God. God can bring finances beyond what you are trusting for in the natural. Move into the supernatural!

The same way you got saved is the same way you get healed and that you get financial increase. The same principles of faith work in praying for your spouse. Don't say, "My husband is never going to change. He is so hardheaded. God will change, before my husband will change!"

Why confess what you don't want? Why not say, "Father, I believe Your Spirit is working in my husband. His heart and mind are being renewed. He is a loving, godly man. He

54

loves to give. He loves to serve. He is a man after Your heart, Father."

When someone says, "How is your husband doing?" you can respond, "God is at work in him. The Lord is doing good things in my husband." Why not say that, because you will have what you say. If you don't say what you want, you're not using your faith. You're simply stuck in your circumstances!

Faith Is the Substance

Hebrews 11:1 says, **Now faith is the substance of things hoped for....** Many people think that hope is the same as faith, but they are different. Faith is the substance of what you are hoping for. You can have hope, but it never becomes tangible. It never manifests in reality. You have your hopes, but they are never brought into substance.

Hope means that you think or wish that someday something will happen. "I have hope for a brighter tomorrow." "I have hope that maybe I'll get healed someday." Or, "I have hope that someday I can have my own house." Or, "I hope that I'll get a better job." Hope has no substance.

Hopes and dreams are part of Christianity, but without faith they will never become reality. Faith is the substance of what you are hoping for.

Speak Your Faith!

Okay, so you're hoping for a company of your own. You want to start your own business. Put your faith to work by saying, "I'm starting my own company. I'm an entrepreneur. I'm getting the money right now to start my own business, and it is going to prosper." Name it because whatever you call it, it's going to come into existence. Speak to it!

"Well, Brother Treat, how can I be sure this will work?" If you were sure, you wouldn't need faith. That's why you call it faith. You are trusting God. You are believing God when in the natural there is no way to know. You don't need faith for the things that you know. You need faith for things when there is no way in the natural for them to come into manifestation.

If you are living a life that doesn't take faith, I guarantee, you're not in God's will. Here's why: God always calls you to a job, to a destiny, to a career that you can't do without Him. So if you get up every day, go through your motions, and do your thing and don't need God, you are outside the will of God. I get up every day and say, "Lord, are You up yet? I can't even leave this bedroom without You." Everything I'm trying to do, I can't do without Him.

Recently we sat down with the architects and builders and drew out our new sanctuary, the youth church, children's church, and the big foyer. Then they started totaling it up. We spent $30 million just like that! Then I said, "Let's pray!" Actually, they wanted to spend a whole lot more, but I said, "My faith is at about $30 million." I can't do that without God.

If you are living in a world where you've got everything all figured out, you can handle it, you can deal with it and you can do it, you're not in God's will. "I'm a self-made man. I pulled myself up by my own bootstraps." You're not in God's will because you don't even need God.

There is going to be a day when you will need faith, when the disease has no medicine for it, when the circumstances have no natural solution, when you're facing a supernatural problem and you need a supernatural God with a supernatural answer. If we walk by faith every day, then we are ready for any day.

Faith is the substance of what you are hoping for, the evidence of what you can't see.

Verse 3 of Hebrews, chapter 11, says: **By faith we understand the worlds were framed by the word of God, so that things which are seen were not made of things which are visible.**

God took His faith and His Word and spoke the worlds into existence. He said, **"Let there be light, and light came into being"** (Genesis 1:3). **"Let there be a firmament in the midst of the waters, and let it divide the waters from the waters..." and it was so** (vv. 6,7). **"Let the waters under the heavens be gathered together into one place, and let the dry land appear;" and it was so** (v. 9). God spoke the grass, herbs and fruit trees into existence. Genesis, chapter 1, repeatedly says, **And God said...and it was so.** He spoke man into existence, and you showed up!

You are going to create your world just like God created His – with your faith. Believing and speaking. You are going to create your home, your career, your car and your friends with the words of your mouth. You literally frame your world with the words you are speaking.

If you look around at your world and you don't like part of it, take a look at what you've been saying. Change what you've been saying. Create a new life. You are made in the likeness and image of God, so use your faith.

You see, faith isn't just a warm, fuzzy feeling whenever you think about religious things. Faith is what is coming out of your mouth to change circumstances. Jesus said it will change trees and it will move mountains. The point is, what you are believing and speaking will change anything in your life.

Hebrews 11:6 says, **But without faith *it is* impossible to please** [God].... God wants you to be out there where you don't know how to do something and where you can't do it on your own – where you've got to trust Him. He wants you to be where you've got to pray and say, "There's no other way to make it through the day!"

But without faith *it is* impossible to please *Him*, for he who comes to God must believe that He is, and *that* He is a rewarder of those who diligently seek Him, Hebrews 11:6.

Someone says, "Well, God doesn't heal everybody." Notice what they are saying. Why don't you believe God is a rewarder of those who diligently seek Him? "Well, God doesn't want everybody to be blessed." Come on, man, stop saying that junk! You heard that from some potbellied preacher who never read his Bible! God wants everyone blessed. He is a rewarder of those who diligently seek Him, and when you use your faith, it pleases Him.

"Well, I wouldn't want to pray for that. I'd be asking for too much." You can't ask for too much from God. He can spare it! He can afford it! Come on, use your faith. It pleases Him.

In Matthew, chapter 8, the centurion came to Jesus to seek healing and deliverance for his servant. Here is my translation of what the centurion said: "Lord, don't even come to my house. Just speak the word and my servant will be healed" (vv. 6-9). Scripture says the Lord marveled (v. 10). Jesus was excited about the centurion using his faith. He said, **"Assuredly, I say to you, I have not found such great faith, not**

even in Israel!" (Matthew 8:10). The centurion was just a soldier!

The Lord wants us to trust Him, step out and believe Him for greatness. Use your faith. How do we know when we're using faith? By what we are saying.

Matthew, chapter 9, verse 2 says: **And behold, they brought to Him a paralytic lying on a bed. And Jesus seeing their faith, said to the paralytic, "Son, be of good cheer; your sins are forgiven you."**

After a discourse with the "religious" scribes, Jesus spoke to the paralytic, **"Arise, take up your bed, and go to your house." And he arose...** (vv. 6,7).

This account wasn't about "this is your lucky day" or about God's sovereignty. It was about faith. Jesus saw their faith.

Many times Jesus walked by the guy who was paralyzed for thirty-eight years. Jesus was around thousands and thousands of sick folks when He walked in His flesh, and many of them didn't get healed. He could only deal with people who believed.

So often we say, "If I had been there with Jesus, I would have received my miracle." If you can't get it now, you wouldn't have gotten it then. I know we don't want to believe that, but it's true. If you can't get it now while the Holy Spirit is in your spirit, you couldn't have gotten it back then when Jesus was in His flesh.

Your Faith Can Change Your Destiny!

Many people have been trained to believe that they are at the whims of life's circumstances. We have put it into our way of speaking. They say things like, "How is life treating you?" That gives the impression that life is in control and you are putting up with whatever comes your way. The Bible doesn't teach that. Life doesn't treat me. I treat it!

It's up to you to decide the level of life you want to live at. You decide how you are going to live emotionally and financially. You decide within the sphere of your calling and destiny and gifting from God. You decide where you are going to go and how you are going to live. Use your faith. Change those circumstances. Speak to that tree. Move that mountain. Don't sit around saying, "Well, life has treated me badly. I was dealt a bad hand." Bluff! There is a way to win, even with a bad hand! Use your faith!

Micah, Tasha and Caleb Exercise Their Faith!

As a young boy, I was raised around horses. Mom and Dad were rodeo folks and we were always messing around with the horses, so they trained us how to deal with them. One of the things they always said was, "You are in control. You decide what the horse is going to do."

A horse is an animal and he will always try to do his own thing. If you let a horse do his own thing, all the training and discipline will be lost and the horse will be out of control. You are to stay in control.

There is a biblical side of it. You have been given dominion over the horse. Remember in James, chapter 3, verse 3, where James said that to control our words is like putting a bit in the horse's mouth? You can control the whole horse if you'll control his mouth. You can control your whole life if you'll control your words.

My kids – Micah, Tasha and Caleb – used their faith to get a horse. Since I was raised with horses, I've been trying to stay away from them, but the kids were confessing, "We're getting a horse." Every night they would pray, "Thank You, Father, for our horse." It was their faith, not mine, that brought a manifestation of the answer to their prayers.

A pastor friend from Idaho called me up and said, "Casey, the Lord spoke to me and told me I'm supposed to give you a horse." I'm thinking, "Great! That's just wonderful!"

He brought the horse. We've got the arena and the stall. Now we are training our kids what to do with the horse: Here's how you put the bit in its mouth. Here's the saddle. Here's how you handle the cinch, and all the various aspects of riding. I'm teaching my children what my parents taught me: You've got to be in charge. You can't let the horse tell you what to do. You tell the horse what to do.

Micah is seventy pounds or so, Tasha and Caleb weigh a little more, and the horse is 1,600 pounds. Micah says, "Okay, Dad, I'm in control."

When you control the mouth, you control the whole horse. So here's a little kid on top of a great big horse and he's making the decisions where to go.

You're in Charge of Your Own Destiny!

Now, you may feel like a tiny person in the midst of a great big life, but you've got the reins because you've got the Word. Speak the Word and go where you want to go. Use your faith. Decide where your life is going to go. Decide how you are going to live. Don't let your life take you back to the barn. Take the reins of life by using your faith.

Remember, faith isn't a feeling. It's a decision to believe and speak the Word, and when you do that you will start changing your circumstances. Faith is one of the key ingredients in your Leadership Matrix.

CHAPTER
SEVEN

Energy

*Since we are filled with the Spirit of God
we should show energy, enthusiasm and fire.*

A leader stays "up" and lives by the energy of the Holy Spirit. A leader doesn't have to get prayed up. He stays up. He doesn't try to get fired up. He is always fired up. A leader is born of the Spirit, filled with the Spirit and walks in the power of the Holy Spirit every day.

Now, that doesn't mean that we need to have a bubbly, outgoing, expressive personality. Whatever your personality and however you express yourself, God needs you to be energized – not discouraged, depressed and feeling like a victim. Not living below the cloud, having a bad day, or being in a bad mood. You can be "up" in the Spirit all the time.

You Have the Power!

In Acts, chapter 1, Jesus talked to His disciples about being "up" or empowered all the time.

[Jesus] **commanded them** [His disciples] **not to depart from Jerusalem, but to wait for the Promise of the Father, "which," He said, "you have heard from Me; for John truly baptized with water, but you shall be baptized with the Holy Spirit not many days from now"** (Verses 4,5).

In other words, Jesus was saying to His disciples, "Don't leave town without the baptism of the Holy Spirit." The disciples had walked with Jesus for three and a half years, but they still were not ready to walk out each day of their destiny until they were filled with the Holy Spirit.

If all the disciples, Jesus' mother, Mary, and Paul, Luke, Silas and every other apostolic leader of the New Testament needed to be filled with the Holy Spirit, so do you and I. Every believer needs to be baptized with the Holy Spirit.

In Acts 1:8 Jesus said, **"But you shall receive power when the Holy Spirit has come upon you; and you shall be witnesses to Me...."** The Greek word for "power" as it is used in this verse is *dunamis* – dynamic, mighty, miraculous power.

Notice the result when the power of the Holy Spirit comes upon you: **"You shall be witnesses to Me in Jerusalem, and in all Judea and Samaria, and to the end of the earth"** (v. 8). That means in your city, in your state or province, in your country and to the ends of the earth.

We are God's witnesses. Why? Because the power of God's Spirit lives in us. We are not down, discouraged, afraid or depressed like the rest of the world. We don't wake up every morning trying to get ourselves going, staggering through half the day until we get energized with caffeine. We're not driving to work with a sick, sad, sorry look on our faces, mad if anyone gets in our lane. Come on! We're not dragging into the office, saying, "I've got a headache. I was out late last night. What are we doing?"

You shall receive power when the Holy Spirit has come upon you, and His power in you will be a witness to the world. The world needs to see Christians who are energized with the power of God.

How can you say you have something people in the world don't have, if you are just as depressed as they are? Just as discouraged? Just as tired? Just as afraid? If you have the same fears, the same worries, the same cloud and the same depression as the world has, but you say you are born of the Spirit and filled with the Spirit, there's something missing! Usually it's not that we don't have it, but it's that we've never learned to live and walk in the power of God.

Continually Filled

In Ephesians 5:18 Paul said, **And do not be drunk with wine . . . but be filled with the Spirit.**

There should be something coming out of every believer – an energy, a life, a flow of God's presence – that causes the world to ask, "What's up with you?" When you walk in the office, everyone knows you are different. When you go home at night, you are different. I mean, you just wake up happy!

Years ago Wendy and I did a ministers' conference in another state. It was one of those conferences where the speakers went on and on.

I was supposed to be the first speaker, then there was a second speaker after me, but before me another preacher was going to receive the offering. Many times when preachers get together, they all have to impress each other. It really gets to be a scary deal!

65

The offering went for an hour, and while they were taking the offering, the host, a friend of ours, leaned over to me and said, "Could you cut your message down to fifty minutes?" I said, "Sure, no problem."

Another ten minutes went by and he leaned over, "Could you cut your message down to forty minutes?" I said, "Sure, no problem." The guy kept on, so the host leaned over to me again and asked, "Could you cut your message down to thirty minutes?" I said, "No problem."

Finally, I got my chance! What had happened during the offering was that the preacher was talking about how hard the ministry was, how discouraged he thought we all were, how we were all experiencing *burnout* and that we needed to stand together because of the pain and the pressures of ministry.

I had prepared a message from John, chapter 4, verses 34 and 35, where Jesus said:

> **"My food** [My sustenance, My energy, My meat] **is to do the will of Him who sent Me, and to finish His work. Do you not say, 'There are still four months and then comes the harvest'? Behold, I say to you, lift up your eyes and look at the fields, for they are already white for harvest!"**

By the time I got up to speak, I was so fired up, and I only had twenty minutes. They said I could have thirty, but I took twenty minutes to preach what I had planned to present in an hour. So I kind of exploded! I said, "How in the world can you be born of the Spirit and filled with the Spirit and sit around burned out? Did God burn out? Did the Holy Ghost get old? Did you lose the power of God?" I didn't realize what I was saying. I just went off.

Recently, as I was cleaning up my office, I plugged in a videotape. It happened to be that message! I sat there and listened and preached myself happy!

I began to realize that Christians accept the spirit of the world quicker than they do the Spirit of God. We allow the discouragement, the depression, the problems and the doom and gloom of the world to affect our attitude. We watch more *CNN* negative news than we spend reading the New Testament, which is Good News! We take on the attitude of the world, so we're down and just hanging in there. We're trying to make a living and make it through!

Even ministers get into this: "Dearly beloved, we are gathered together to share our depression." But when people come into an environment where the Spirit of God is, where the music is up, where the people are lifting up their hands, their voices and their eyes because they are lifting up their heart to the Lord, people say, "What's happening?"

If you will get energized and let the Spirit of God flow out of your life, you will affect people. They will not be able to forget you. Ten years later, they will be saying, "Remember when you walked into the office and you touched me and prayed for me? I've never been the same since."

Do you want to lead, make a difference in the world and have a positive impact, or are you going to be one of the depressed people droning through the freeways of life? I'm not saying you need to have the same personality as every other person. But don't walk around under a cloud. Don't be sad-faced and depressed. I've seen people sitting in our church after we have worshiped and praised the Lord, and they never crack a smile. I mean, ceramic faces! You need to get up! You need to get yourself loosed and delivered from depression, because until you do, you *are* a cloud. Not under a cloud, but you are the cloud!

Stir Up the Gift That's in You

In Second Timothy 1:6, Paul said to Timothy, **Therefore I remind you to stir up the gift of God which is in you through the laying on of my hands.** Why would Paul have to remind Timothy to stir it up? Because it can get lost under the fears, the worries, the anxieties, the problems, the negative circumstances and the negative people. And if you're not careful, that gift of God, that power from God, that presence of God can get buried under *CNN*, under fourteen hours a day of sitcoms, under thirty-seven pages of bad news reports, under problems at the office, under fights with your spouse. Pretty soon everything God has put in you is buried. Paul says, "Stir it up! Stir up the gift of God that is within you!"

If we opened your life up and all we saw was the yogurt, if we'd stir it up, we'd find the fruit! Come on! Stir it up!

God Didn't Give You a Spirit of Timidity

Second Timothy, chapter 1, Verse 7 says, **For God has not given** [you] **a spirit of fear….** The Greek literally says, "God has not given you a timid spirit." Why don't you witness to that person at your office? Because you are timid. Why don't you go to your neighbor and say, "Let's go to church for Christmas this year"? Because you are timid. Why didn't you stop your Thanksgiving dinner and say, "We're going to spend a few moments just praising God"? Because of the spirit of timidity on your life. Paul says, **…stir up the**

gift of God…. The Lord didn't give you a spirit of fear, **but of power, love and a sound mind** (2 Timothy 1:6-7).

The motivation is: Do we love people? I don't have time to worry about my image, or be afraid of what you think about me. I don't have time to be worried about who I might offend. I don't have time to be concerned about the relatives who might not like it. God didn't give me a spirit of fear, but He put power, love and a sound mind in me. Why? *So I can make a difference in people's lives. I want to make a positive impact on people's lives.*

I love the story I heard from one of our ushers. They had their family over for Thanksgiving and most of them aren't saved. They started talking about the Lord and they said, "Let's talk about the things that we're thankful for." Everybody started sharing and in the midst of their giving thanks, it was obvious that there was a lot of pain. So our usher said, "You know, the Bible teaches that God heals broken hearts. We can anoint you with oil and pray for you and the Lord will heal you today."

They got out the oil. I don't know if it was Crisco or what. It doesn't matter. Right there on Thanksgiving afternoon, they anointed their family members with oil. These people weren't even saved, yet they were asking God to heal them.

Pretty soon Grandma got born again. They had revival on Thanksgiving. Why? The love of God got them through their fears, their timidity and their thoughts of, "What will they think of us?" It's time to stop worrying about what someone thinks about you, and start thinking about someone else. God put His power in you. Get energized and let that power flow out of you.

Work Out Your Own Salvation

The last phrase of Philippians 2:12 says, **Work out your own salvation with fear and trembling.** In other words, with a holy awe and respect for God, we must work out, bring to completion and live fully this salvation. Don't take it for granted. Don't pull out your salvation once a week when you go to church. Work out your salvation on a daily basis.

You have muscles, but if you don't work them out, they will hide underneath the fat! Muscles atrophy for lack of exercise. If you don't work them out, you can't use them to accomplish all that is possible. I mean, you can't even get the jar of grape jelly opened, because your muscles haven't been worked out. But if you will exercise them, they will tone up and develop and you can use them to do all kinds of things.

Paul says, **Work out your own salvation,** because your salvation will energize your life. It will empower your life. It will bless your life. But if you let it hide under the fat of selfishness, you won't be able to open up what God has for you.

The Amplified Bible says of this verse, **Work out (cultivate, carry out to the goal, and fully complete) your own salvation....**

Then verse 13 in the New King James Bible says, **For it is God who works in you both to will and to do for His good pleasure.** Another translation says, **To act and desire according to His good pleasure.** The Amplified Version of this verse says, **It is God Who is all the while effectually at work in you [energizing and creating in you the power and desire], both to will and to work for His good pleasure....** I love those words. God is energizing and creating in us the power and the desire to do His good pleasure.

I get up every morning thinking, "God is working in me. God is energizing and creating in me power and desire to do His will," rather than, "Oh God, I've got to go to work again."

What do you suppose would happen to your day if you would start thinking that God is energizing and creating in you the power and desire to do His good pleasure?

Emotions Follow Thinking

Many people don't realize that their emotions follow their thinking. Emotion doesn't cause thinking. It follows thinking. So if you are blah and down and I walk up to you and get you thinking on something good, suddenly your emotions come up. Or you might be feeling pretty good and I come up to you and give you something negative to think about and your emotions go down. Your emotions will always follow your thinking. **For as he thinks in his heart, so is he** (Proverbs 23:7). When you think good thoughts, your emotions are up and you have energy. But when you think bad thoughts, your emotions are down and you feel tired, depressed and discouraged.

A little boy couldn't get out of bed. He was too tired and he said, "Dad, I think I'm sick." The next day Dad says, "We're going fishing at 4:00 in the morning." So at 4:00 the next morning, the little guy is standing beside his dad's bed with his clothes on and his fishing pole in his hand. "A miracle happened, Dad. I got healed!" Both of these responses from this little boy are based on thinking.

If you get out of bed thinking, "Man, I've got to go to work. I've got to go on the freeway again. I've got that lazy secretary, or I've got that lousy boss. I've got all these problems," you are going to be hitting the snooze button as many times as you can. You're going to crawl out of bed, stagger to the coffeepot, drive to work and you're just another sad face slipping into the office at the last minute. Yet you say you are baptized with the power of God.

That night you drive home from work and your spouse greets you with, "How was your day, Honey?" "Oh, Fine." You're reading the paper. "I love you, Honey." "Yeah, sure, me, too." You wonder, *What's happening?* You have allowed the standard of the world, the energy level of the world, the oppression and depression of the world to become your norm. You think it's normal, but it's not. It's because of the way you are thinking that your energy level functions that way. You act like everyone else acts because you are thinking just like everyone else thinks.

But if you got up thinking, *God is working in me and energizing me and creating in me power and desire to do His will,* you wouldn't need the snooze alarm.

So why is the snooze on/off button so big? Because the manufacturers know you're not going to do what you said you're going to do. They know that you don't plan to get up when you say you're going to get up. They know you're going to start your day compromising, faking on yourself, lying to yourself and you don't really want to get up. You've got to play games for fifteen or twenty minutes to talk yourself into it.

By the way, why do they call it an "alarm clock"? I thought alarms were only for fires, disasters, floods, air attacks and problems. Why do you need an alarm to get out of bed? When you walk in these ingredients of vision, strategy, relationships and faith, you certainly won't need an alarm, and you won't need a snooze button!

I'm not saying that if you've been through time zone changes or maybe you were out late or something special, that you won't need the alarm to make sure you don't sleep in. But I'm talking about normal life. You should be up and moving with desire, because God is energizing you and creating in you power and desire to do His will. You don't need a clock to scare you out of bed. And you don't need to lie and compromise for fifteen minutes while you try to get yourself moving. You've got life on the inside of you. Stir it up and let that energy of God motivate you!

When this energy begins to flow out of you, then your neighbor is going to say, "You know, I've never seen you down. Do you ever have a down day?" You say, "I think I did one time back in 1983, but it only lasted a minute because I've been baptized with the Holy Spirit. Ever since then I've had energy flowing on the inside of me."

At your workplace people will say, "How come you are kind when people treat you bad?" You say, "I have energy that's beyond what most people have. I don't need to have a cocktail to relax, and I don't need some pills to get me excited. I don't need drugs to have a party. I have energy flowing on the inside of me."

It's by Anointing!

I will never forget when I first met Spirit-filled Christians. I watched them to see what kind of drugs they were using. I tried to figure it out, because whatever it was, it was good and I wanted it. They had good things going on.

Then they told me, "No, you don't smoke it. You don't shoot it. You don't eat it. You don't drink it. You get filled with it." I said, "Go ahead, do that to me." You see, this isn't a game. It isn't a joke. It is real. To be born of the Spirit and to be filled with the Holy Spirit is real. The power of God comes on the inside of you.

You need to let that energy flow out of you everywhere you go. While in that grocery store line, you need to say to the checker, "I appreciate you doing such a good job with all these people. You have been really special, just hanging in there. I'm proud of you!" He or she will just look at you like you're from Mars because the last person was griping about a bruise on their tomato!

The energy of God will make you a leader in every aspect of your life. You will have positive impact on people and they will ask you, "How do you do that?" You will say, "It's God. I am born of His Spirit and filled with His Spirit. The power of God lives in me and His energy flows through me. Every day I am up; I live up because God is in me!"

EIGHT

Follow-Through

We must continue to show up
until we outlast the devil.

A good leader will follow-through and outlast the enemy. A good leader is still standing when the enemy gives up. He will still be standing strong when the devil gets tired and goes home. A good leader never quits. He never stops. He doesn't fail. He follows through until he wins!

First Corinthians 13:8 says, **Love never fails....** One translation says, **Love never stops....** Usually you won't fail if you won't stop. I think many of us are living below God's best and living without His blessings, not because we are doing wrong things, but because we stopped doing the right things. We gave up too soon. If we are going to experience God's best in our lives, we have to follow-through.

A good leader doesn't think short term: "How can I get where I want to be this week? This month? This year?" A good leader thinks about a lifetime. We're not thinking that when we hit forty, the end of our life is near. Or at fifty, we are getting tired. Or at sixty, we're going to retire. No, good leaders follow-through. We're going to live this thing until we are 110- or 120-years-old (Deuteronomy 34:7). We are going to live this life long enough to establish God's will, to fulfill His plans, to finish His work and be the people that He created us to be.

The world thinks:

- Get rich quick. How can I get what I want now?

- I don't want to get married. Let's just have sex.

- I don't want to fulfill my contract. If I don't like it, I'm going to negotiate.

- I don't want to follow-through on my word. I'll do whatever I feel like doing today.

Today many people can't follow-through. That is why they are wracked with failure.

You and I are supposed to be different and follow God's plan. Part of that plan is long-term thinking and long-term follow-through.

Hang on to Your Confidence!

Hebrews 10:35 says, **Therefore do not cast away your confidence, which has great reward.** Isn't it strange that God would have to say to us, "Do not cast away your confidence"? I mean, why would anybody cast away their confidence? If you start with confidence, why would you cast it away? Obviously, it's an issue or God would not have spoken about it. The fact is, many people start good, strong and with confidence. We are good at starting strong, but not finishing strong.

We grab that ball of yarn and knit up a storm. Yet that project has been in the closet unfinished for the last seven years. Or we got all excited about finishing the basement. We went out and bought the lumber, got our hammer and it has been piled up in the basement since we moved in four years ago.

We get excited about a new class and we tell everybody, "I'm going back to school to get educated." On the third assignment, we give up, we drop the class and fail to finish it.

Or we are excited about our marriage relationship. We stood at the altar and said, "Until death do us part," but we were just kidding. What we meant was, "Until I don't feel like it," because we think we've lost the love for our spouse.

Many of us cast away our confidence, and when you're not confident about what you're doing, you won't finish. You won't stay on course. You won't endure. Paul says, "Don't cast away your confidence."

Verse 36 of Hebrews, chapter 10 says, **For you have need of endurance, so that after you have done the will of God, you may receive the promise.**

Christianity isn't a sprint. It's not a short-term race. It's not a ten-second blast. It's a marathon. Come on! You don't have to be fast, but you do have to stay in the race of life. You don't have to be a sleek gazelle. In the Christian life, the turtle can win and the hare can be beaten. The key is endurance.

You can get a bad start and still have a great finish. The sprinter has to get out of the blocks perfectly, because if he doesn't leave the starting blocks perfectly, there's no way he can win the race.

But for the marathon runners, it's not that big a deal. The marathon runner can start late. The marathon runner can be tying his shoes, grabbing a drink of water, talking to his friend and when the gun goes off, he says, "Okay, I've got to run now," because he knows the start is not the issue. He's got 26.2 miles and that guy who was leading the race in the first ten yards is probably not going to be leading at the end. The guy who was so excited and started with a great burst of energy is probably not going to feel that way after about twenty miles.

In fact, Jesus said, "There are many who start out like a flash in the pan, with all kinds of great things happening, but they don't last. They have no roots. They are shallow. At the first sign of a test, a trial, a difficulty or a challenge, they vanish away" (Luke chapter 8, my paraphrase).

The ingredients of perseverance, endurance and patience must be included in the leadership matrix. Without these qualities you will not have the ingredients to fulfill God's will. You will fall short of God's best for your life. Now, this is not the way the world operates, but it is the way God operates. These qualities are necessary for your success.

Do not cast away your confidence, which has great reward. For you have need of endurance, so that after you have done the will of God, you may receive the promise (Hebrews 10:35,36).

Persevere!

You see, it is possible for people to do the right thing but not get the right results because they quit too soon. Many people do the right thing for a while. They stay holy for a while. They stand for righteousness for a little while. They give their tithes for a week or two, maybe even a month. They obey the Bible for a little bit. But then they get weary because they don't see the results fast enough, so they begin to think, "What good is this? I want it now. I'm not getting what I need today." They give up on it. They don't endure. They did the will of God for a season, but they didn't endure and so they never saw the promise.

The Lord is concerned with what happens *in* you, not just around you. You're praying for these things to happen, but God is watching your attitude, your character and your maturity. He is waiting to see what you are made of. So you did the will of God for a season, but then you did not receive the promise because you didn't endure.

Patience! Patience! Patience!

James 1:2-4 says: **My brethren, count it all joy when you fall into various trials, Knowing that the testing of your faith produces patience. But let patience have its perfect work, that you may be perfect and complete, lacking nothing.**

All of us want the end of that verse – **perfect, lacking nothing** – but we don't want the stuff that comes before it! We all want to lack nothing. We all want to be perfect and complete and mature. The King James Version says, **entire, wanting nothing**. I want that! I want to be in the place where I am entire, complete, whole, lacking nothing. All that I want and all that I need, I have it. I want that. But I hate the other part – **count it all joy when you fall into various trials**. That's a bummer!

And **knowing**. Who wants to know? Who wants to have to think and use the brain that God gave you? **Knowing that the testing of your faith produces patience** (v. 3). That's not fun! **But let patience have its perfect work, that you may be perfect and complete, lacking nothing** (v. 4). This is a process that God is very concerned with. God watches over our lives in these areas. When we get into these trials, how we handle them lets the Lord know whether we are ready for Him to answer our prayers or not. How we deal with the trial, the test, the problem, the situation, tells the Lord whether He should go ahead and get us out now, or just let us simmer a little longer.

What do you do when your child has bad behavior and you discipline him or her? You watch to see how they deal with the discipline. If they are stomping, whining, griping, complaining, slamming the door, sticking their lower lip out and acting like their dad (or whoever!), then you think, "Okay, I need to give him more discipline," or "I'm just going to let him sit in that for a while." Right? Apparently they're not getting it yet. They still have their little attitude and rebellion. They are still thinking, "It's not fair. It's not right. I can't believe you did this to me." As a result, you just leave them in it.

They may be on restriction for another couple of days, or they may be assigned to some special work around the house, and you let them simmer in the discipline. You're not concerned about what is happening around them. You are concerned with what is happening in them. If their attitude, the rebellion and the disobedience aren't being changed, then they are in trouble and they are going to grow up to be an adult with lots of problems.

So the Lord allows us to get into situations on the job. He puts a demon-possessed person in the desk next to yours! Right? You know what I'm talking about. He moves you into a neighborhood where everybody around you is crazy and weird. He puts you on the freeway next to a guy whose only assignment is to see if he can bug you. The Lord just does that, not because He wants evil, but because He wants to see what's in you. He wants to see that you are who you say you are. You said you are a Christian. He wants to see an expression of His character being developed in you. Many times satan comes with problems, but the Lord uses it to make us better.

Now, if you're still flipping people off and shaking your fist, the Lord says, "Obviously, it's not working in them yet. They don't have it." When you get into a difficulty with your marriage and you're pouting, stomping and slamming doors, the Lord says, "They're not getting it yet."

When you're in a difficult situation at work and you're griping, gossiping and talking about the boss, the Lord says, "Obviously, they're not growing. My child needs longer restriction, because he's missing the point." The point is not only the situation you're dealing with. It's what is happening in you while you deal with it. If you know that, it's just a matter of your faith being tested. It's a matter of counting it all joy in the midst of the trial. It's a matter of developing your patience because you know it will make you better, bigger and more like the Lord.

So you can say, "Okay, go ahead, turn up the heat. I'm going to take another lap while I swim in the boiling water of these circumstances."

The Lord says, "I'll answer their prayer, because they've got it. I'll change that circumstance because they've got it. They have learned. They have grown. They have gotten everything out of that situation they can get, so I'm going to go

81

ahead and bless them, prosper them, deliver them and answer the cry of their heart." At this point, you are perfect and entire, wanting nothing.

If the Lord bailed you out of every test before you passed it, how foolish would that be? So often in our short-term attitude – "I want it easy. If it's tough, I'm going to quit" – we bail out of the problems, we quit the job rather than learn from it, we run from a relationship rather than changing, learning and growing to become a better Christian. We avoid the situation rather than use it to make us bigger and better. If that's the case, you will never be perfect and entire, wanting nothing. There will always be lack and problems. You will always be in a circumstance where you're not being fulfilled.

Chill Out and Re-Adjust Your Focus!

Begin to look at the long-term deal. Jesus knew He was going to hang on a cross, but that's not where He placed His focus. Scripture says, **Who for the joy that was set before Him endured the cross...** (Hebrews 12:2).

Okay, so you're going to be on the freeway for a few minutes. Don't focus on that. Chill out. You've got a long-range vision. You may have some problems at the office tomorrow, but don't live for that moment. Look beyond that to what God is saying and doing in your life, to where He's taking you, and count it all joy as you go through various circumstances on the way to where God wants you to be.

If you gossip, complain, gripe, murmur, get depressed, walk around saying, "I'm depressed. Nobody understands me. Nobody knows." With this kind of attitude, the Lord will say, "Just leave him (or her) alone." Angels were on their way to deliver you, but the Lord will say, "Stop, don't touch them.

Leave them alone." The Spirit of God was present, but the Lord said, "Hold back. Just let him (or her) finish their song!"

The answer, the provision and all that God wanted you to have was on its way to you, but because you didn't count it all joy, you didn't know that the Lord was trying to develop some faith and patience in your life, and you didn't deal with it biblically, the Lord cannot respond to your needs. As soon as you begin to grow spiritually and you are on your way to becoming the person God wants you to be, He will come in and do supernatural things on your behalf.

God wants to bless and prosper your life, but He is more concerned with what is happening in you than what is happening around you.

Good Things & God Things Take Time

Nothing good happens fast. Good relationships don't form as a result of a one-night stand. It takes time. A good relationship takes weeks and months and years of communication. Good marriages don't happen in a year or five years or even ten years. Good marriages take a lifetime of learning and growing and patiently enduring one another.

Wendy and I have been together over twenty years now. Even for me it has been twenty years of learning about myself, figuring out how I think and why I feel certain ways about certain things. Now, if it has taken me this long to learn about myself, and I'm actively pursuing understanding, think about the average person who spends more time watching television than anything else. How are they ever going to know themselves? Or how will they ever know their spouse?

After twenty years, I'm just beginning to know myself. I'm starting to know Wendy. She's beginning to know herself. The next twenty years are going to be better. I'm really convinced that it takes at least twenty years to build a foundation for your marriage relationship. Then in the thirtieth, fortieth, fiftieth and sixtieth year, you really start celebrating and enjoying one another. It just gets better in the spirit, in the soul, and in the body, too. That means that even sex gets better.

Many of us are so short-term in our thinking. The average marriage in America doesn't make it to the foundational level. We go through the honeymoon and the years of trying, seeking and wondering, then we give up.

Nothing that is good happens fast. Great things take a long time. A beautiful, deep, hard wood takes years to grow. We don't want to wait that long. Just give me some of that particleboard and I'll glue it together!

Good food takes hours to prepare. They don't put the good stuff in a paper bag and throw it out the window at you! You have to sit down and after you place your order, then they begin to cut your meat and prepare your salad. That's the good stuff! You've got to sit there while they go through the process. That's how you learn about your wife.

If you want your food in a bag through the window, then there is no process. You don't have to learn. You don't have to wait. Just get it now!

This is part of the problem with our "modern mentality." We want everything quick and that circumvents God. God doesn't wear a watch. He doesn't keep a Day-Timer. He isn't nervous about a schedule. He will wait, because He knows you aren't going anywhere.

We have to begin to change our way of thinking and learn how to develop endurance and patience. Those qualities in our leadership matrix will take us where we want to go.

It's an amazing thought to me – in fact, it kind of boggles my mind. The average pastor changes churches every four years. It's very difficult to teach the members of your church about commitment and endurance if you move every four years. The congregation members are going, "Yeah, you tell me. I've been here longer than you, and I'll be here when you're gone." That means that even among ministry leadership, endurance, patience, faithfulness, consistency and long-term commitment are very scarce. Our whole world is that way. We've got to break that spirit and change that mentality. I've been pastoring my church for more than twenty years, and I have no plans to move.

"Never, Never, Never Give Up!"

When the great Winston Churchill, who led the allied forces of Europe and America through World War II, was invited to speak at a college graduation, he studied, prepared and meditated. He thought, "What can I impart to these young college graduates?" The graduates, alumni, parents, families and friends were excited that Winston Churchill was to speak to them. As he was introduced, he slowly walked to the pulpit. People sat on the edge of their seats to hear this man. He said these words: "Never, never, never give up!" Then he sat down. That was it! End of speech!

The people thought, "You've got to be kidding! I want something cool. Revelation. Wisdom. Insight." Yet that speech has never been forgotten. It has been quoted as much as any other, and possibly it has had more impact than anything else he could have said. The truth is, *you will win so many battles if you don't give up!*

When Wendy and I communicate with each other, we come from different perspectives, different points of view. (Sometimes it takes her a while to realize how right I am!) When we are discussing and trying to sort through our differences, there are many times when I don't know what to say or I don't know what to do. I'm trying to understand and she's trying to understand. I don't have a clue and neither does she. At times we have said to one another, "Well, let's just keep talking. Something's going to come out." Don't quit! Don't give up!

The only difference between the end of our argument and the end of many couples' arguments is, we don't leave the room. We don't slam the door. We don't hang up if we're on the phone. We don't quit. Sometimes that's the only difference between winners and losers – we don't quit!

Does it mean anything that you are leading the game at halftime? Not really. Is it cool that you are leading the game at the third quarter? It doesn't really matter. The issue is, who wins the game when the clock runs out.

Maybe you've lived a holy life for ten years, then you committed adultery. Those ten years are shot. You tried to build your marriage for seven years and then you said, "Forget it." Seven years are gone. Rarely do we say, "Isn't it great that the team hung in there for almost the whole game?" No, we just say, "They're losers." Right? You don't consider that they almost won. You simply focus on, "They lost."

We don't say, "They almost stayed married." No, we say, "They got divorced." Now, divorce isn't the unforgivable sin. Don't get me wrong. I'm just saying, many of these kinds of failures are simply because you quit. You didn't have any problem that others haven't faced. You didn't have an issue that was unique – exclusive to just you and you alone. You didn't have a circumstance that couldn't be dealt with. You just quit.

There are times when one person quits and leaves and the other wants to make it work, so I'm not condemning anyone. I'm just trying to teach the principle of follow-through. We've got to outlast the devil. We've got to keep praying, believing, renewing, staying and enduring until the end. Then we'll have the victory!

You see, we've got folks in church who don't even want to endure a 90-minute service. I mean, our services are short. We have twenty minutes of praise and worship; fifteen or twenty minutes of prayer, giving and special music; then thirty or thirty-five minutes of the Word. We've got people running out the back door while we're praying for lost, dying people. They can't even stay through the altar call.

If we were going for four or five hours and it was boring, I'd run too. I'd escape. I wouldn't come. But when you can't sit still for ninety minutes, pray for lost people and intercede for folks to get help from God, something is wrong.

I know that some people have jobs and responsibilities they have to attend to. That's another deal. I understand that. But a lack of faithfulness, a lack of follow-through, and a lack of patience is a curse. If you want God's blessings, the curse must be broken. The Lord is not going to respond to you simply because you put His plan in your Day-Timer. He's going to watch your spirit and your heart and see what is working in you.

Finish It!

In John, chapter 4, Jesus sent the disciples into Samaria to get some food. When they came back, He was ministering to a woman at the well. They were surprised that He was talking to the woman. They said, **"Rabbi, eat"** (v. 31). **But He said to them, "I have food to eat of which you do not know"** (v. 32).

The disciples said to each other, **"Has anyone brought Him anything to eat?" Jesus said to them, "My food is to do the will of Him who sent Me, and to finish His work"** (vv. 33,34).

Don't you love that word "finish"? Jesus was saying, "The food that I eat, the thing that energizes Me, the nutrients of My life, the vitamins of My work, the thing that sustains Me, is to do God's will and *finish* His work."

Remember, as Jesus hung on the cross, the last thing He said was, **"It is finished!"** (John 19:30). Aren't you glad He didn't quit before He finished His work?

What about you? Are you going to finish? What has God put in your heart? Are you going to finish what you said on your wedding day? Are you going to finish the vision that's inside of you? At the end of your life, will you be able to stand before your Father and say, "It is finished"?

We live in a world where many of us don't finish. We've got to break that cycle. We've got to teach our kids by example, "Whatever you start, finish. Stay on the team until the end of the season, even if you don't play." We're to be like Jesus and finish what we start. Our meat is to do the will of God and finish it. Come on, let's finish!

In Second Timothy, chapter 4, verse 7, Paul said, **I have fought the good fight, I have finished the race, I have kept the faith**. If you follow-through and finish what you start, you will experience God's blessings. Then, one day you will stand before the Father and He will say, **"Well done, good and faithful servant"** (Matthew 25:21).

What's important isn't how quickly you get your first million – or how quickly you get your first luxury car. It's about *finishing, following through, being faithful*. Then, at the end, you will be just as strong or stronger than you were at the beginning.

Lord, help us to be like You. Help us to be Christians who follow-through, who endure, who finish what You put in our hearts to do. Thank You, Lord, that You are working in us. We will let patience have its perfect work in us so we can be perfect, complete and entire, lacking nothing.

NINE

Renewal

We are never there,
but always in the process of becoming like Jesus.

Thus far in this book we have discussed the following leadership matrix ingredients or characteristics that will enable us to be the kind of people God has called us to be as examples or models for others:

- Vision

- Strategy

- Relationships

- Faith

- Energy

- Follow-Through

In this chapter, we will conclude with the important ingredient of *renewal*.

If you will begin to think like a leader, you will rise to the level of life God has called you to. If you think like a survivor and act like you're just trying to make it through life, you will always live on a lower level of life than what is possible.

If you develop these characteristics in the leadership matrix, your life will be meaningful, purposeful and productive. That's what God wants for you.

It is not God's plan for you to get saved and then suffer and struggle through life until you go to heaven. I don't know where that concept came from, but it did not come out of the Bible. The will of the Lord is not for you to become a Christian, stop doing everything that's fun and just hope Jesus comes back quick so you can go to heaven. That's not Christianity. That's some kind of religious mentality or traditional thinking that does not come from the Bible.

You Can Make a Difference in Your World!

The Bible teaches a lifestyle that is influential, one that changes the world around you and produces results. It is fruitful in relationships, finances, creativity, joy and fun.

People in the world look to sex, drugs and material things in an attempt to find happiness, joy and fulfillment. But God wants His people to live on a level of joy, peace, creativity and productivity that influences and affects the world around us.

As Christians, we're supposed to be the lights. When you turn the light switch on, you should be able to tell a difference. If you walked into a room, flipped on the light switch and nothing happened, you'd immediately say, "Something's wrong. Either somebody unplugged the lamp or the light bulb is burned out." You turned on the light, but there was no change.

Christians often walk into offices and there is no change. They walk into businesses and there is no change. They walk into relationships and there is no change. Many times Christians walk into church and nothing happens. The lights don't come on. There is little or no productivity, creativity, influence or effect on the world around us. It's not because we're not saved. It's because we haven't thought like leaders and put the proper ingredients to work in our lives.

As Christians, we believe in God, but we don't believe like God. Even the world and Satan believe in God. But we, as Christians, are *to believe like God.* We are to think like God and possess His thoughts and attitude, which will reveal His character and lifestyle to those around us. That's what Christianity is all about.

Renewal: A Continual Process

As leaders we must renew our minds and lives continually with the Word of God. To renew something means to take what is old and give it back for something new. When you renew your driver's license, you turn in your old one and you are given a new one. Now, if you don't have something old, you can't get something new. It's an exchange. When you renew your life, you are releasing the old and bringing a new way of acting, thinking and living into play. So it's an exchange – a divine exchange.

Genesis 1:2 says, **The earth was without form, and void; and darkness was on the face of the deep. And the**

Spirit of God was hovering over the face of the waters. God began to move and create. As a result, change, growth and newness began to happen.

So how do you know when something is alive? We look to see if it is moving. How do you know if a plant is alive? It's growing, expanding and changing. If you are alive and growing, then you will be moving, changing, increasing and bringing new things into your world. In Genesis, chapter 1, the Spirit of God moved, created and things happened. Nowhere does it say that God stopped.

The natural, human tendency is to find a comfort zone and stop. Most of us, once we get through the years of education, try to find a place where we can get comfortable and stop. If we stop learning, moving, creating and bringing forth new things, we're moving closer to the cemetery!

Our ministry doesn't exist to help people be "comfortable." If you're going to church just so someone can pat you on the head, make you feel good and keep you saved until you go to heaven, then there are many other places to do that. Some churches are designed to make you feel good. Their leadership says, "You're doing good. Hang in there. Jesus is coming back soon, then we'll all be in heaven!"

Our goal is not to give you a comfort zone of survival, but to help you become like Jesus. The Bible says you were predestined to be conformed to the image of Jesus Christ.

Transformed to Be Like Jesus

Romans 12:2 says: **And do not be conformed to this world, but be transformed by the renewing of your mind, that you may prove what is that good and acceptable and perfect will of God.**

I believe this verse is the crux of the entire New Testament, the fulcrum of all New Testament teaching. It's the key verse to everything Paul said and everything that the New Covenant stands for.

If you want to be in God's perfect will, you must renew your mind, which will cause *transformation* to take place in your life. The end result is, you will no longer be like the world.

You won't be renewed and transformed just because you listen to sermons, read Scriptures, or show up at church. It happens when you purposefully change the way you think, and that's a very difficult process because you have to work through your defensiveness. You have to work through your insecurities. You have to work through your desire to cover up your foolishness or your mistakes.

It's easier for a child to be transformed than an adult because they don't have to be defensive. They don't have to act like they already know everything. They don't have to cover up for their lack of knowledge. A child is open and able to learn. Each day is new to them. Each day is exciting. They have much more energy, not because of the size of their bodies, but because of *the attitude of their minds.*

As adults, we tend to spend so much mental time and energy defending, thinking bad thoughts, worrying and going through the negatives that children don't go through. They have energy because they are focused on learning and experiencing and living. To them, everything is new and exciting.

Sometimes around eighteen, nineteen, twenty, or twenty-four, we stop thinking that way and we start acting like, "I'm an adult now and I know what's going on. I've got it together. You can't tell me anything, because I already know." We become defensive and insecure and we develop an attitude, which makes it difficult to learn. Or, we learn technical data, but it's hard to learn things that will cause us to change our attitudes, our personality, the way we think and believe.

I'm not talking about learning a new computer program. I'm talking about learning something about yourself and something about God that will change your life.

We have brilliant people who can learn all the computer science and other information, but they can't change one thing to make their marriage work. We have brilliant people in the world who have so much knowledge, but they can't change one attitude to improve their relationships with people.

You may be brilliant with knowledge in your field of expertise, but you can't make one change so you can parent your children to success in life. That's the kind of renewal that it takes to get to God's perfect will. As you are transformed by the renewing of your mind – not just learning – you will have God's perfect will.

Put on the New Man

God wants us to be like children. In Matthew 18:3 Jesus said, **"...unless you are converted and become as little children, you will by no means enter the kingdom of heaven."** What did He mean by that? Does He want us to be immature? No, He wants us to be able to learn and not just gather more data. He wants us to be renewed so we can change the way we think. If we are not like little children in the ability to learn, there will be many things in God's Kingdom that we will never experience.

Colossians 3, verses 9 and 10, say, **...put off the old man with his deeds... put on the new man who is renewed**

in knowledge….

When we speak about the Christian life, seldom do we say, "You have to get *new knowledge* to live the Christian life." Usually we say, "You've got to have *faith*, read your *Bible* and go to *church*," which are good things to do. But Paul said, **Put on the new man who is renewed in <u>knowledge</u> according to the image of Him who created him** (Colossians 3:10).

So to live the Christian life, you've got to get new knowledge, think differently and renew your mind so you can experience God's perfect will.

Recently, Micah, who as I write, is in fourth grade, had a basketball game. Usually fourth graders don't know a lot of the basketball skills. They just show up and put on their uniforms, with the tank tops sliding off their skinny shoulders and their pants pinned so they'll stay up because they don't have any hips! And, of course, they're wearing their *Jordan* shoes. They might bounce the ball a couple of times and run, then take a shot, but it doesn't even get up in the air! The ref does a good job, but he overlooks many things. He just lets them play. About the only time he blows the whistle is when there's blood!

What do we say at the end of a fourth grade game? "Good game! Man, you're a good player! I mean, you were doing great!" And they don't even know what the score is! "Yeah, we won!" And it was 12 to 2 in the opponent's favor.

When you are ten-years-old, you just show up and everything is cool. But you can't play that way when you're in high school. By then you need more skills and a better understanding of the game. You've got to be able to run plays and take shots.

It's good when you first become a Christian to show up at church. It's good that you put in your $5 offering and think you're really doing God a favor. It's good that you sit with your arms crossed and with your funky attitude, wondering, "How long is the service going to go?" It is good that you simply show up!

But when you've been a Christian for several years and you're still going through the same motions, you still have the same attitude, the same income, the same relationships, the same vision and the same spirit, it's not good anymore. In fact, it stinks!

As a pastor, it's my job to challenge you and give you the biblical material to help you become more like Jesus. No one is 100 percent like Jesus, yet. If you think you are, you have several major problems! We have a long way to go. Romans 8:29 says we are predestined to be conformed to the image of Jesus Christ. That means every day we must be in the process of renewal, not just gathering data, but changing the way we think, being renewed in knowledge to think like God thinks. The end result is to do His perfect will.

Learning, Growing, Changing

You may be in God's perfect will today, but if you don't keep learning and growing and changing, you're not going to be there tomorrow. What's good for a fourth grader isn't necessarily good for a twelfth grader. We want progress and forward motion.

We need to be actively involved in changing anything that's not like Jesus. Jesus controlled His flesh, so we need to make some changes to bring our flesh under control. If we can't build relationships – intimacy, openness and honesty –

with people like Jesus did, then we need to make some changes. If we're not prospering financially so we can give and take care of multitudes like Jesus did, then we need to make some changes.

You may never be a millionaire, but you should have financial resources to give and make a difference in the world. That's what Jesus did, and we are predestined to be conformed to His image.

First John 4:17 says, **...as He is, so are we in this world.** This kind of life isn't about waiting until we get to heaven. It's about living like Jesus here and now on the earth. We don't need more of Jesus in heaven. We need more of Jesus on this rotten old sinful earth. That's life.

So how can we become more like Jesus? Our normal thinking is, "I have a problem sharing because my dad was a real quiet guy, and I didn't grow up in a house where we shared. I have a problem with that, so get off my case." That's not a biblical attitude. The *biblical attitude* is, "I never had good relationships. I've never had a good example. But I want to be more like Jesus so I'm going to open up and share. I'm going to open up and be honest."

The *natural attitude* is, "I inherited this genetic problem. My dad, my mom, my race, my culture and my nation had it, so that's the way I am." The *biblical attitude* is, "I've got all kinds of problems from my family, but Jesus bore my sicknesses and carried my diseases. I am renewing my mind. I refuse to live with sickness. I live in divine health. I am becoming more like Jesus every day."

We defend and excuse many of the world's attitudes, but the Lord says, "Don't be conformed to that. Be transformed by the renewing of your mind." We will always be on our way to being transformed as we purpose in our hearts to renew our minds with the Word of God.

Renewed Like the Eagle

Psalm 103 says in verses 1 and 5: **Bless the Lord, O my soul; and all that is within me, bless His holy name! Who satisfies your mouth with good things, so that your youth is renewed like the eagle's.**

Your youth is renewed. The word "renewed" in the Hebrew means exchange. There is a divine exchange that takes place as we give up our old ways of thinking, and take on God's way of thinking. I'm giving up my old excuses and I am taking His truth. I am giving up my old defensiveness and I'm taking His openness. I'm giving up the way the world is and I'm taking on the way heaven is. I don't want to be conformed. *I want to be transformed.* My youth – that open, honest, able and willing-to-learn-and-grow-and-change attitude – is being renewed in me again.

One of the greatest examples of the renewal process to Wendy and me was the life of Dr. Lester Sumrall, founder of LESEA International. When Wendy and I met him, he was in his sixties. He died when he was in his eighties. Lester Sumrall used to pull me aside and say, "Now, don't let those old people mess things up around here." I said, "Brother Sumrall, you are old." He'd reply, "I am not. *Old has nothing to do with age, but it has everything to do with attitude.*"

In his eighties Brother Sumrall was still flying all over the world to preach the gospel in a different country almost every week. He was a great man. He never got old, he just stayed young.

Second Corinthians 4:16 says: **Therefore we do not lose heart** [become discouraged or depressed]. **Even though our outward man is perishing, yet the inward man is being renewed day by day.**

That inward man – the spirit and soul on the inside of the body – is getting younger every day. Come on! Let's make a concerted effort to stay open, not to get old and crusty or closed, and not to have a funky attitude about the things that aren't the way we would like them to be.

I remember driving down the street in my car and my kids put in a CD. I thought, "What kind of noise is that? I can't even understand the words. Do they have to have it so loud?" In the midst of it, I had a flashback. I saw myself sitting in my mother's car, putting in an 8-track tape, and my mom saying, "What kind of noise is that? I can't even understand the words. Do you have to have it so loud?" Suddenly, I realized I was becoming a little closed!

Go After *All* God Has for You!

Most of us receive one revelation from God and we die with it. In other words, we have one insight, one vision of what God wants to do with our lives, one idea of what Christian life is all about and we stay with it. We live our lives with it and we die with it. Consequently, church history is full of churches that had a revelation or a revival. They got excited about it and grew to a peak. Then, the leadership got old and they didn't know how to change or how to renew their minds, so it died out.

Young people leave a church like that; they scatter, or they might become involved with a new movement. But that church just goes down. That's exactly what happened to a

101

church where Wendy and I attended. It grew and peaked out. When the pastor died, a handful of old people sat around and talked about the way things used to be.

So the history of the Church is this up and down thing – 2000 years of going up and down. Why don't we get up and say, "I'm going to hand the baton to someone and I'm going after another revelation"?

Brother Sumrall said to me, "Most people never get a second revelation. They die with the first one." Let's get a new revelation. Let's learn something else about God. Let's find something new that the Lord wants to do in our lives. Let's don't peak and go down. Let's take another step up. We can go from glory to glory to glory if we will keep learning, changing and staying fresh.

A revelation soon becomes our destination. Then it's our denomination. Then it's our institution. Then it's crystallization. When you become crystallized, you are so hard that the Lord can't do anything with you. The only way out of crystallization is to get melted! That's when you need the fire of the Holy Ghost.

We don't want to get stuck in that cycle. We want to stay young and have our youth renewed. I'm not talking about age; I'm talking about attitude. Though our outward man is getting older, our inward man is being renewed day by day.

In Lamentations, chapter 3, Jeremiah is talking [or lamenting] about the mercies and compassion of the Lord. He says of God's mercies and compassion, **They are new every morning; great is Your faithfulness** (v. 23).

You see, God doesn't get old because He rarely does anything the same way He did it before. Yet He never changes. Malachi 3:6 says, **For I am the Lord, I do not change....** Hebrews 13:8 says, **Jesus Christ is the same yesterday, to-**

day, and forever. So how can He be new every morning, yet never change? It has to do with spirit and attitude.

As an example, when you first came to church you were excited about the Lord. You wanted to learn the Bible and find out more of what God could do in your life. But ten years later, why are you going to church? It has become a ritual or a tradition. You're no longer motivated for life and newness. Now, it's just the thing to do.

When you first had a baby, you took that child in your arms and you went into the throne room of God and prayed, "Father, thank You for this child." By the time he or she is five years old, it's changed to, "Lay down. We're going to pray." Now, you're just going through the routine. There is no more life. It is not new anymore. What God does is never because of what He did yesterday. What He does is because He is God and what He does is new every morning.

Stay fresh. Stay new. Stay excited. How come young Christians can bring so many more people to the Lord than older Christians? Partially because they know more people who don't know the Lord, but after you've been saved for many years, most of your friends are Christians. But that's not the only reason. I believe it's even more so because young Christians are excited about God. Some of us who have been saved for a while have lost the newness.

When you open a bag of potato chips and you leave them in the cupboard for six months, they have all the same ingredients that they had originally. Maybe a couple new ones!! It's still the same potatoes, the same salt, the same grease and the same preservatives. But they have lost their crispness and freshness. They are the same, but they are stale. So what do you do with that bag of chips? You throw it away!

There are Christians who are born again, they are baptized in the Holy Spirit and they believe the Bible. They have all the ingredients, but they are stale. There is no crispness. No freshness. They're not thinking, "Who am I going to bring to the Lord this year? How am I going to get my family to church this year?" What does the Lord do with lukewarm people? Revelation 3:16 says, **...because you are lukewarm, and neither cold nor hot, I will vomit you out of My mouth.**

Let's stay new and fresh. Let's keep learning and growing. In your leadership matrix, you're going to have a serious deficiency if the component of *renewal* is missing.

The work of God is new every morning. Make sure you stay with Him. Be willing to make changes, take the steps and go for that new thing that God wants to do in your life.

Father, help us not to get stale and simply go through form and routine and ritual. Help us to be new every morning by Your Spirit, becoming more and more like Jesus every day so we can make a difference in our world. Amen.

Author's Teaching Notes

LEADERSHIP MATRIX

by Casey Treat

Matthew 12:35 "A good man out of the good treasure of his heart brings forth good things, and an evil man out of the evil treasure brings for the evil things."

Ephesians 5:15-18 (AMP) Live purposely, worthily, accurately.

- Matrix = (womb) within which, or from which something originates, forms and develops; a mold, die or impression for manufacturing.
- Leadership is the controlling factor in the growth and multiplication of your influence.
- Leadership is always the problem and always the answer.
- When leaders do what God has called and gifted them to do, people will follow and numbers will increase.
- Leadership is a gift that is received, as well as a skill that is developed. Divine + Human, Super + Natural
- COMPASSION – leaders are moved with compassion for people in all that they do. THIS IS THE OVERRIDING MOTIVATION OF ALL WE DO. Mark 1:40,4; 1 Corinthians 13:1-4; Galatians 5:6 (AMP)

I. VISION – leaders start with a vision of where they want to go, what they want to build, what they will accomplish.
Joshua 6:1,2; Proverbs 29:18; Acts 2:14-17; John 4:35

   A. The vision of a true leader is a passion that consumes his life.
John 2:17; John 4:34-36

    B. A leader carries vision in his spirit and soul 24 hours per day, 7 days a week – not just at new year planning meetings.

    C. Your vision is the blueprint you are building.

    D. Your vision is your future.

    E. Your future is in your heart.
       Matthew 12:35

II. STRATEGY – leaders develop a strategy of how they are going to go, build and accomplish the vision.
Proverbs 3:13-19; Proverbs 4:5-8; Matthew 9:35-38; Acts 6:1-7; Acts 5:42

    A. Vision is what you are going to do, strategy is how you are going to do it.

    B. Strategy must be born from wisdom and knowledge.
       Proverbs 3:19

    C. Strategies come from teams of skilled people adding their expertise to a game plan that produces growth and victory.

    D. Strategies include:

      1. Schedules, time lines;

      2. Focus and targets;

      3. Marketing and advertising;

      4. Budgets and fundraising;

      5. Synergy with other projects;

      6. Goals and measurable results; and

      7. Review.

III. RELATIONSHIPS – leaders build relationships with mentors, peers and followers to accomplish their vision.
Proverbs 13:20; Proverbs 11:14; Luke 9:28 (with 3); Luke 9:1,2 (with 12); Luke 10:1 (with 70)

    A. Your relationships will move you forward or hold you back.

      1. Every staff member must help you fulfill the vision.

      2. A staff member that isn't hurting you, but isn't helping you, will eventually hurt you if you give him enough time.

    B. Leaders know who to release and no longer relate to.
       Genesis 13:5-17; Acts 15:36-40

       1. God would not speak to Abram again until after he had separated from Lot.

       2. What is God going to do in your life when you get your relationships cleaned up?

    C. Many leaders avoid intimate relationships because they are too insecure in their roles to accept confrontation or challenge. Proverbs 9:7-9

IV. FAITH – leaders take the risks, trust God and inspire others to use their faith.
Matthew 8:6-13; Mark 11:22-24; Romans 1:17; 2 Corinthians 5:7

    A. God will always require you to walk by faith, not feeling, emotions, etc.

    B. Faith comes from the heart through the mouth and causes natural things to change.

    C. Faith moves the hindrances and overcomes the obstacles.

    D. God doesn't respond to what you need, want or deserve – He responds to your faith.

    E. If you have "figured out" how to fulfill your vision, you don't need God.

    F. Many leaders seek security, and stop living by faith.

V. ENERGY – leaders keep passion, joy, excitement, and life in every service, project and step along the way.
Nehemiah 8:10; Proverbs 17:22; Acts 1:8; Philippians 2:13 (AMP)

    A. Without the energy and passion of the Holy Spirit, you are left with emotional hype or dead, dry services, staff, etc.

    B. Spiritual life is exciting, religious tradition is boring.

    C. Spiritual life and passion comes from inside the leaders, not from programs, songs or productions.

    D. If it isn't in you, all you can produce is emotional hype that soon gets old and dry.

VI. FOLLOW-THROUGH – leaders are patient, enduring and able to stay the course until the vision is fulfilled.
Hebrews 6:12; Hebrews 10:36-38; 2 Timothy 4:7; James 1:2-4

A. Much of our growth and success comes by simply outlasting the enemy.

B. Christianity is a marathon not a sprint.

C. Find a pace that you and your family can live with for the rest of your life.

D. Jesus and Paul were committed to finish their course.
John 4:34

VII. RENEWAL – leaders are continually renewing their vision, strategy, relationships and themselves.
Lamentations 3:23; Romans 12:2; Colossians 3:9-11

A. Anything that is living is growing, anything that is growing is changing.

B. Creative leadership is normal to those who are called by, filled with, and directed by the Spirit of God – the creator of the universe.

C. Leaders know they must be fresh and new everyday for all ministry flows out of them.
John 7:38,39; Acts 20:28

VIII. WHY PEOPLE WILL COME TO YOU

• You must understand why people come to you, in order to meet them where they are.

• You can only serve a person what they have come to receive.

• When you force more on them than they desire, they become offended and won't return.

• Give them what they came for, and pray their appetite will increase and they'll be back for more.

A. They want to FEEL BETTER today.

B. They want HOPE for the future.

C. They want HELP and HEALING.

D. They want CHANGE and RENEWAL.

E. They want to fulfill their VISION and DESTINY.